The Right to a Carer's Assessment: Exploring the E Learning Disabilities.

Copyright © 2016 by Shingi Sakuringwa

ISBN 978-0-9931361-0-8

Published by:

Ignish Publishing House, Ashford, Kent, UK.

2016

All rights reserved.

Without limiting the rights under copyright, no portion of this dissertation may be reproduced or distributed in any form or by any means or stored in a database or retrieval system without prior written permission of the publisher with the exception of excepts from articles, reviews etc. The recommendations contained in this book are intended to provide informative insights into impact of services provided for carers in a small part of England in the hope that larger scale research by others will test generalizability of the results.

Cover design © by Suraj.

For further information or permission;

IGNISH PUBLISHING HOUSE

www.ignishpublishinghouse.com

ETHICS APPROVAL

This dissertation has been completed using the ethical guidelines for research involving participants as provided by Brunel University Ethics Board. All participants were informed of the details of the study; all participants provided informed consent and have given consent that their data to be analysed and presented in this dissertation. In order to protect the anonymity and privacy of all participants identity has been changed unless otherwise indicated. Any names of persons or places appear as pseudonyms unless otherwise indicated.

ACKNOWLEDGEMENTS

It is with pleasure that I acknowledge the help and support that I got during the period of study for this dissertation. I am indebted to my family, the Carer's Centre management, staff and carers who participated in this study.

My dissertation supervisor provided invaluable support, patience, insight and understanding. I would also like to thank the staff in the School of Health and Social Care, Brunel University for all their assistance.

This book is dedicated to carers all over the world.

Thank you all

ABBREVIATIONS

CA Carer's Assessment;   LD Learning Disabilities

CC Carers Centre   LA Local Authority

TABLE OF CONTENTS

ETHICS APPROVAL 2

ACKNOWLEDGEMENTS 3

ABBREVIATIONS 3

Chapter 1   INTRODUCTION 8

    1.1 Introduction 8

    1.2 Definition of a Carer 8

    1.3 Definition of learning disability 8

    1.4 Background to the problem 9

    1.5 Purpose of the study 10

    1.6 Contribution to research 10

    1.7 Context of the study 10

    Outline of the study 11

Chapter 2   LITERATURE REVIEW 12

    2.1 Introduction 12

    2.2 Research into caring and learning disability 12

    2.3 Literature gap 19

Chapter 3   RESEARCH DESIGN AND METHODOLOGY 21

    3.1 Introduction 21

    3.2 Research design 21

    3.3 Research Methodology 21

    3.4 The Sample and Piloting 23

    Table1. 24

    3.5 Research ethics 24

    3.6 Confidentiality, informed consent, voluntary participation. 25

    3.7 The Instrument 25

    3.8 Data analysis 27

    3.9 Problems encountered in data collection 28

Chapter 4   FINDINGS, ANALYSIS AND DISCUSSION 30

4.0.0 Introduction 30

4.0.1 Results 30

Table 2 Themes 30

Telling their story 30

    4.0.2 Assessment Process 30

    4.0.3 Assessment experience 31

    4.0.4 Assessment impact 31

Self Development 31

    4.0.5 Leisure 31

    4.0.6 Education 32

    4.0.7 Short courses 32

    4.0.8 Work 32

Life on hold 33

    4.0.9 Carers health 33

    4.1.0 Multi role of the carer 33

    4.1.1 Challenging behaviour 33

Coping Strategies 34

    4.1.2 Care Sharing 34

    4.1.3 Religion 34

Formal Services 34

    4.1.4 Respite 34

    4.1.5 Worry with community Access 35

Discussion 35

Telling their story 35

    4.2.0 Assessment Process 35

    4.2.1 Assessment experience 36

    4.2.2 Assessment impact 36

Self Development 38

    4.2.3 Leisure 38

    4.2.4 Education 39

    4.2.5 Short courses 40

    4.2.6   Work 40

Life on hold 41

    4.2.7   Carers health 41

    4.2.8   Multi role of the carer 42

    4.2.9   Challenging behaviour 44

Coping Strategies 46

    4.3.0   Care Sharing 46

    4.3.1   Religion 47

Formal Services 48

    4.3.2   Respite 48

    4.3.3   Worry with community Access 49

    4.4.0   Purpose of the study. 51

Chapter 5   CONCLUSION AND RECOMMENDATIONS 53

    5.1 Introduction 53

    5.2 Consideration of research limitation 53

    5.3 Ideas for further research 53

    5.4 Conclusion and recommendations 54

        Telling their story 54

        Personal development 54

        Life on hold 54

        Coping strategies 55

        Formal services 55

REFERENCES AND BIBLIOGRAPHY 56

    APPENDIX A: The instrument 74

    APPENDIX B: Participant Consent form 75

    Appendix C   INFORMATION SHEET 76

    Appendix D   Consent from the Carers Centre 78

    Appendix E   Transcript 03 79

    Appendix F   Ethics approval 85

    Appendix G   Colour coded Transcript 88

    Appendix H (a) Thematic data reduction 92

- (b) Code Threading into major themes 93
- TABLES of results 94
  - Table 3: Assessment process 94
  - Table 4: Assessment experience 94
    - Participant 94
  - Table 5: Assessment Impact 95
    - Participant Assessment impact 95
  - Table 6: Leisure 96
    - Participant Sub-theme: Leisure 96
    - Table 7: Education 97
    - Participant Sub-theme Education 97
  - Table 8: Short Courses 98
    - Participant 98
    - Table 9: Work 99
    - Table 10: Carers' Health 100
    - Table 11: Multi role of the carer 100
    - Table12: Challenging Behavior 102
    - Table 13: Care Sharing 103
    - Table 14: Religion 104
    - Table 15: Respite 105
    - Table 16: Worry with community access 107

Chapter 1   INTRODUCTION

1.1   Introduction

This chapter sets the scene into the research. It gives definitions, discusses the significance of carers and outlines the research purpose and structure. The European Union estimated in Europe in 2005 that about 19 million carers cared for 20 hours per week and 9 million for 35 hour or more per week, (Glendinning, 2011). They estimate that by the year 2030, 21 million will be caring for 20 hours and 11 million for 35 or more hours per week. These are staggering figures for a 'largely hidden resource,' Glendinning, (2011), carers. Quereshi et al (1998), believe that the family is the main unit within which care is provided and that there has always been an uneasy relationship between the family and the state.

1.2 Definition of a Carer

The 1995 Carers' Act defines a carer as; 'one who gives substantial amount of time to caring.' The National Family Carer Network (NFCN) details characteristics of a carer as one who; supports a person with disabilities with daily living activities; safeguards, holds vital information on the individuals history; takes legal responsibility; provides continuity in transitions; advocates; is the eye and ear for the individual; picks up pieces when things go wrong; knows the individual's subtleties in communication; helps in money matters and staff recruitment; even if that individual has moved away from home, (NFCN). These characteristics encompass what Beresford et al (2005) summed up from research findings with carers and service users, 'care is what people who love you do,' and because of that, this study will use the NFCN definition of carer; ' a person who is not paid to have a personal, continuous relationship with a person with a learning disability,' (LD).

There are 6,440,713 carers in the UK of whom 5,246,325 are in England, the majority of whom are women, (Carers UK, 2011).

1.3 Definition of learning disability

The UK is the only country which uses the term LD, others use 'intellectual disability' and for this reason, this study will use the term LD. The Equality Act (2010) defines disability as mental/ physical impairment which has substantial long term adverse effect on ability to perform normal day to day activities. LD is a state of arrested or incomplete development of the mind, (WHO).

The Human Rights Act (1998) has a list of capacities for day to day activities and say that an impairment affects normal day to day activities if it involves at least one of the capacities; mobility; manual dexterity; physical coordination; ability to lift and carry; speech/hearing/sight; memory and ability to concentrate/learn /understand; perception of risk or physical danger. The British Psychological Society states that LD is a neurological disorder affecting the brain's ability to receive, process, store and respond to information; it has 3 core criteria, significant intellectual impairment; adaptive/social function; and onset before adulthood. This study will use the definition by Valuing People (2001) White Paper, 'learning disability includes the presence of significantly reduced ability to understand new or complex information to learn new skills; reduced ability to cope independently ; which started before adulthood and has lasting effect on development.' This is consistent with WHO ICD-10. 1 in 220 children in the UK have LD, (Carers UK, 2011). Classification of LD into moderate, severe and profound is made on the basis of intellectual functioning, social functioning and the support required, (SEN).

1.4   Background to the problem

Carer recognition and the development of services to meet carers' needs evolved separately from policies for disabled and older people, (Twigg and Atkin, 1994). The legislation which brought care into the community was the National Health Service and Community Care Act 1990 (NHSCCA, 1990) and as a result most institutions were closed. Section 47 of the Act placed a duty on Local Authorities to assess people who need 'regular and substantial care' and this led to the burden of care being placed upon the informal carers. Five years later, in 1995, the Department of Health (DH), Carers' (Recognition and Services) Act was implemented which gave carers the right to request an assessment. However, there was no guarantee that they would receive a service as there was no money set aside by the Government to provide services, (Robinson and Williams, 2001).   This presented a major challenge for practitioners as they were asked to conduct Carers Assessments, (CA), without the resources to offer services, (Robinson and Williams, 2001).   In addition, they found interpreting 'regular and substantial' problematic (Robinson and Williams, 2001). However, the Carers and Disabled Children Act 2000 entitled carers to a service for their identified needs. This Act was followed by the Carers Equal Opportunities Act 2004 which placed a duty on professionals to take into account Carers' desires to work and to access education and leisure.   The NHS Performance Framework (2005), have two standards, C14 and C 17, which stipulate that carers should have suitable and accessible information about services and the complaints procedure; and requires that organisations take account of views of carers in planning and delivering service. With the 2014 Care Act, Local Authorities have a duty to assess and meet the needs of the service user and carer. Local Authority assess the impact of caring on the carer's well-being and achieving desired outcomes. Carers do not have to be providing substantial and regular care but have to meet an eligibility criteria in areas of well-being and outcomes.

1.5 Purpose of the study

Carers receiving CA had downward trend from 1998 when it was 38% to 25% in 2002 (Princess Royal Trust, 2002). In England, around 353,000 carers received an assessment during 2006 - 2007, of whom 315,000 received a service, Glendinning et al (2009). The purpose of this research is to find out how carers experienced the CA process and how the services have impacted their lives. Two research objectives form the basis of this study;

- Exploring the experiences of Carers for people with learning difficulties who have had their needs assessed and have received service.

- Exploring whether the support/ services received by the carers are meeting their needs.

1.6 Contribution to research

It is envisioned that the results of this study will inform practice for working with Carers of people with LD. This research will contribute to the body of knowledge on the experiences of carers of people with LD who have been assessed and how the services they have received have impacted them. It will make contribution to the social work profession by informing practice and provide valuable insight for social workers who work with carers of people with LD. This research will make an original contribution to the profession. It is an indirect assessment of how practitioners are fulfilling the main roles in social work of availing information to carers to be able to make informed decisions and how they provide services. My research will find out from the Carers who receive a service how practitioners deal with the dilemmas of assessment, budgetary constraints and expectations of carers. For the carers as service users, it offers a platform to advocate on behalf of the people they care for. The study will address the gap in community access to more information generated from carers by a carer, the researcher. The study will extend understanding of perspectives of daily living for carers and cared-for forming a positive working relation by identification of a way forward from the carers.

1.7 Context of the study

This research was carried out at a Carers' Centre, (CC), in North London which has been serving carers for 20 years. The CC provides advice and information to carers on benefits, grants etc and has many activities for their social inclusion. It publishes a monthly newsletter which is sent to more than 2800 members. The CC provides advocacy, appeals for benefits and general support of carers including arranging outings and applying for grants to meet carers' needs.

Outline of the study

The study collected primary data during face-to-face semi-structured interviews which were be recorded. This study is divided into 5 chapters: Chapter 1 is the introduction.

Chapter 2 reviews and critiques existing literature on LD, carers, caring and shows the literature gap.

Chapter 3 gives information about the methodology, instrument used, sampling, data collection procedures and problems faced in data collection.

Chapter 4 discusses the results (tabulated in the appendices), analyses the results in the light of literature reviewed and discusses the implications of the findings.

Chapter 5 makes conclusions and recommendations for practice.

Chapter 2   LITERATURE REVIEW

2.1 Introduction

This chapter is about evidence based research on caring and LD. It deals with what is known from extensive evidence-based research on carers covering stress in carers, older and sibling carers, respite services, carers' health, carers' coping strategies and the burden of care. It also deals with major issues relating to people with LD, challenging behavior and community access. In this chapter, the gap in literature is highlighted and it forms the basis for this research.

2.2 Research into caring and learning disability

Carers have received much research attention, (Van Excel et al, 2008) as they contribute significantly to the social care model, (McNally et al, 1999). Twigg and Atkins (1994) identified four groups of carers; a resource, a co-worker, a co-client and a super ceded carer. The burden of care falls on women although current research suggests men are catching up (Carers UK 2011). Most carers have other responsibilities in addition to caring (Deimling 1992).

People with LD may have additional physical difficulties such as posture problems, problems eating and drinking, constipation, incontinence (NHS Executive 1999) and other problems such as depression and mental health. This triad of impairments can affect social communication, social imagination; social relationships (Wing and Gould, 1979) and they change over time. Wing (1981) indicate there is a high prevalence of males with LD.

Melville (2007) conducted a cross sectional study using an interviewer administered questionnaire with 63 carers on their knowledge and perceptions of public health recommendations on diet and physical activity. Although the study was conducted with paid carers, it found that people with LD had a higher prevalence of obesity and showed this to have a significant contribution to increased health needs (Janicki, 2002) which are often unmet

(Lennox & Kerr, 1997). According to Emerson (2005), adults with LD lead physically inactive lives which impact negatively on their health. Health is a state of complete physical, mental and social well-being, (WHO). Health may include physical' mental, emotional, social, spiritual and societal health and it is a personal and societal concept (Tait and Genders 2002). It is worth noting that the UK Government strategy for health of the nation does not include spiritual health, (Tait and Genders 2002). People with LD may develop mental health problems, although it is debatable whether they are more vulnerable than the general population, (Hatton 2002). Little research has been written on families and carers of people with LD who have a mental health problem, (Grasta et al, 2006).

Research by Young et al (2007) used a qualitative approach, incorporating semi-structured interviews with 20 people with mild LD, 10 carers and 10 care workers. Data were analysed using Miles and Huberman's five-fold process. They concluded that people with LD have become increasingly exposed to health risk with the move to living in the community. Research by Dew et al (2004) proved death of a family member has devastating impact on people with LD and because of them losing their parent carers, they could become very isolated as few of them get married, (Dew et al, 2004).

Many older parents live with adult children with LD, (Weekes et al, 2009). And this is associated with higher dependency needs (Roberto, 1995). Leininen (2011) found that most carers help family as part of their retirement but would like to devote time for other personal interests. Kuupelomaki et al (2004) did qualitative study involving 4 European countries comparing data with a survey involving 290 carers in 3 towns in Finland. Their aim was to explore coping strategies used by carers looking after older adults at home. Although this research was not specifically about carers of people with LD, it showed that there are similarities and differences in coping strategies for carers in different countries. Carers in Britain felt they got more professional support and that faith based organisations was a greater source of support unlike carers in Sweden. However, in both countries, carers pursued their own outside interests. Llewellyn et al (2010) did research in Australia with older parent carers and their aging of their children who had LD. Their conclusion was that most carers use self-reliance as a coping strategy and this presents a challenge for service providers as the service offered do not have much impact on carers' lives.

The sibling relationship is ascribed and remains part of one's identity (Cicirelli, 1995). The literature on sibling carers highlights the concerns of negative impact of being forced to 'grow-up too quickly' (Abrahams, 2009) and that some siblings express rage or shame in their relationship with their disabled sibling (Abrahams, 2009) while other siblings develop skills for coping (Dyson, 2010). Some literature on siblings has shown that some non-disabled siblings shy away from caring because of the care taking activities, (Cuskelly & Gunn, 1993). Other studies, for example, Boyce and Barnett (1993), show that siblings value personal qualities of the cared-for and they care for the sibling when parents pass on, (Jewell & Stein, 2002; Williams et al, 2010). Sisters tend to provide on-going support as the strongest sibling bonds are between sisters and same gendered sibling dyad. These have stronger ties than cross gender dyads (Orsmond & Seltzer, 2000). Sibling support is different from parental support in mostly providing social contact, recreational activities and standing in for the parent in administrative issues,

(Smith et al, 2000). The Strozier (2012) study used the Dunst Family Support Scale (Dunst et al, 1994) to measure the impact of kinship social support groups. Although the study is based on kinship support groups and not linked specifically with LD, it recommended more evidence-based studies to understand informal kinship carers about who little is known.

Practical daily tasks of caring for people with LD are described as limitations that affect quality of everyday life and can have significant emotional impact on the carer (Heron, 1998). The stresses and strains, or 'daily grind' (Stalker, 2003) are also associated with the carers' third shift, 'care worrying,' Hochschilds (1997). Challenging behavior has been associated with care burden (Nachshen et al, 2002; Savundranayagam et al, 2011). The Carers' health is a stressor (Heller & Factor, 1993) which affects the caring ability; although in different studies it has been used as a resource, (Heller et al, 1997) and as an outcome (Epel et al, 2004; Seltzer et al, 2001). Research by Leggett et al (2010) focused on carer isolation, age, service user age and formal service use. Their findings highlighted the burden experiences of carers from the impact of daily living activities, recurrent behavior and emotional problems.

The Department of Health and Department of Work and Pensions sponsored the Survey of Households 2009-2010 as part of UK government's Carers' Strategy program in England. Face to face interviews were held with 2401 carers identified by multi-stage stratified random sampling. They found that carers are poor, struggle with their own health but they are reluctant to institutionalize. Hirst (2004), found that carers who are co-resident with the cared-for are more at risk of psychological distress; that carers who provide more than 20 hours of care a week are at greatest risk of poor health and adverse health changes. Research by Buyck et al (2011) in France, the Gazel Cohort cross sectional study, involved 10687 men and women aged 54 to 70. It explored the relationship between caring and improved self reported physical and mental health. Their results showed that regular carers, with a high burden of care, reported worse health status with higher cognitive complaints than non carers; and that caring can have positive effects on health if the caring activities are not too heavy. They recommended that intervention for carers should be multi component and tailored, (Gitlin et al, 2003).

Burton (2006) used a grounded theory approach in Qualitative research to explore the carers' experience. Burton used focus groups with ten carers and also semi-structured interviews with 4 carers of older people. The study concluded that carers' lack of confidence in perceived quality of care from support services was a major barrier for not accessing the support available. The results indicated that not all carers view caring as a burden. They recommended more support services for carers, since the carer's situation tends to impact on the personal, emotional, social, spatial experience of both carer and the care recipient, (Wiles, 2003).

Cheung (2004), used an interpretive phenomenological approach and analyzed the findings in a major theme, 'caring as worrying' where the study found that carers worry about the cared for, their own health, institutional care and lack of support. Several studies on caring (Carers UK, 2005; Jones et al, 2002; Nankervis et al, 1997; Chambers, 2001) indicate that carers get little respite, have poor health, they use positive and negative coping strategies and have anxiety from the inconsistency and irregularity of support. Some parents gave up work to become carers (Weekes et al, 2008; Caples & Sweeney, 2010) some want to work but are unable to fulfill those desires because of the caring demands and inadequate support (Yoong & Karitsas, 2012).

The stresses and strains from 'daily grind' (Stalker, 2003) on carers can be relieved by respite which benefits carers (Catherall and Iphofen, 2006; Wilkie &Barr, 2008). Shaw et al (2009) see respite as any intervention which provides the carer with a break from caring role. For the person with LD, respite is a short break at home, in the community or in a residential setting (Treneman et al, 1997). Mansell & Wilson (2009) carried out research using mixed method approach with 151 carers. They used a questionnaire and focus groups to study carer's perceptions of respite care services offered by their Local Authority. The research concluded that respite did not match carers perceived needs. Mencap (2006) recommended that respite should be frequent, of high quality and enjoyable for both the carer and the cared-for. Mencap (2006) indicated that respite still remains problematic and that 8 out of 10 carers had never had respite and 1 in 3 families had not had a CA. Wilkie & Barr (2008) noted a dearth of literature on respite services and experiences of carers of people with LD; and also that carers want locally based respite, increased leisure activities and home based respite schemes. Respite care has been criticized because respite provision 'system works for the system not the user,' (Power, 2008); for lack of flexibility and poor quality (Wiles, 2003). The results from research lack empirical studies with findings on respite results and benefits (Joen et al, 2005).

Welch et al (2012) did a cross sectional survey using a questionnaire with 239 parent carers and 84 siblings to find the impact of short breaks on siblings. They used thematic analysis of the descriptive data and concluded that short breaks appear to have considerable positive effect on siblings but their current role is unrecognized and undervalued, (Welch et al 2012).

Research into challenging behavior is inconclusive about causes of challenging behavior. Individuals with LD who live at home showed lower rates of behavior problems compared to those in residential living arrangements, (Heller et al, 1997). Emerson et al (1998) state that challenging behavior puts the person displaying it and others at risk, interferes with home life, family members and affects the persons' ability to interact with the community members and facilities. Behavior can be violent, disruptive, destructive, self-harming, repetitive, elective incontinence and may be associated with learning disability (Emerson et al, 1998). In the quantitative study with 66 families by Emerson et al (1998), all children displayed 11.5 different forms of challenging behavior. 7 participants reported that the only useful support came from family members or other parents with similar children and experiences.

McGill et al (2005) found that challenging behavior occurs in at least 7% of people with LD, with increased prevalence in the 15 – 24 year age range. Their quantitative study concluded that most carers were dissatisfied with support and services received and that those with children with challenging behavior do not receive services and support that they find helpful. Minnes et al (2007) carried out qualitative study with 80 adult carers over the age of 50 to explore carer's appraisals of the social support and formal service use and their aging, stress and challenging behavior of the cared-for. That study found that 69% of the individuals with LD were reported by parents to have moderate to severe challenging behavior; and social and formal support systems did not reduce the carers stress. Challenging behavior of people with LD has been found to be a strong determinant of increased care giving burden over time, (Minnes and Woodford, 2004; Lecavalier et al, 2006, Beck et al, 2004). Social support, including family support, is associated with lower parenting stress (Ben-Zur et al, 2005). Parental locus of control has positive impact on the child- parent relationship and minimized likelihood of behavior problems (Hassall et al, 2005). The study by Brylewski & Duggan (2004) proved that medication, which is the main intervention, has limited efficacy. Challenging behavior has significant impact on the carer's emotional life, (Sloper et al, 2006).

Carers are aware of all the subtleties of communication of the person with LD they care for, (NFCN). Watzlawick et al (1967) believe that all interactional behavior in communication has a message value. Bradshaw (2001) speculates that poor communication with service users with LD contributes to 'challenging behaviour.' Rooney

(2002) pointed out the difficulties of being part of a community if you are unable to communicate and concluded that communication is the precursor to social activity. Complex communication difficulties make effective communication one of the vulnerable areas of life, (Cogher 2005). The 'supported decision-making model' (DH 2001) states that all human beings communicate and express choices and 'these choices and preferences are the building blocks of decisions,' (Concannon 2005).

Religious coping is a multi-dimensional search for significance in difficult life events through spiritual means (Pargament, 1997). Positive religious coping views religion and spirituality as being supportive and it is linked to improved physical and psychological coping (Pargament, 1997). Robinowitz et al (2009) explored the relationship between religious coping and cumulative health risks with 256 carers. Although the study was based on carers of elderly relatives with dementia, the findings showed negative and positive religious coping strategies depending on how the carer used religion to cope. There was strong positive association between positive religious coping and positive outcomes for carers. Religion and spirituality are viewed as protective factors against negative, mental health outcomes in the general population (George et al, 2002). Organizational religiosity (church attendance) was inversely associated with depression and complicated grief

(Hebert et al, 2007). Religion has indirect influence on physical health as it promotes positive behaviors and restricts negative (smoking, drug use), (Ellison and Levin, 1998).

Canda (2008) observed that spiritually sensitive practice is attuned to the highest goal, deepest meanings and most practical requirements of clients seeking to nurture clients' full potential through relationships and promote peace and justice. There is mounting evidence that a person's sense of positive spiritual meaning, purpose, connectedness and participation in supportive religious communities are associated with enhanced wellbeing, (Canda and Furman 2010).

It is more difficult to access services for adults with LD than for children with LD (Blomquist, 2006). Carers need a sense of partnership with services and confidence in the services used by the cared-for but there is lack of coordination between service and families (Social Policy Research Unit, 2007). Carers' input is important in providing new services, Seddon & Harper, (2009). Professionals fail to consider the factors related to resilience and focus only on pathological factors (Bayat, 2007). Carers have feelings of anxiety and worry when services were inadequate and inappropriate, (Graungaard &Skov,

2006). Increased social support and increased participation in leisure activities for carers of people with LD were associated with positive appraisal of quality of life (Caples & Sweeney, 2010; Yoong & Koritsas, 2012).

There are limited employment opportunities and poor planning for transition from children to adult services, (Tait & Genders, 2002). Beresford (1995) identified high stress level, lack of finance, poor health, feelings of isolation and breakdown in relationships among carers of people with LD. Hubert (2006) held informal interviews with 30 family carers of adults with LD from Black and minority ethnic communities. They found that even very elderly and ill carers and those caring for people with severe disabilities received little support.

Parent management training programs for behavior management in LD are effective for improving parental well being and parenting skills, (Hames & Rollings, 2009; George & Kidd, 2011) . A pilot study by George & Kidd, (2011) assessed the validity of a modified Incredible Years Parent Training program as intervention for parents of children with moderate to severe LD. They used a pre- and post intervention repeated measures design, observation and self-report measures of perceived stress and behavior problems. The results showed a decrease in stress, and an increase in observed positive interactions. This was only a pilot study and so cannot have conclusive results unless a larger sample over a longer period is used.

Yueh-Chung et al (2011) conducted a census survey in a city of Taiwan with 796 carers of adults (aged 18 or older) diagnosed with less severe LD and those with profound intellectual and multiple disabilities (PIMD). Nonparametric analyses showed that health status, formal social support, and quality of life of carers of adults with PIMD were significantly lower than their counterparts and that these variables were significantly associated with carer educational level, employment status, family income, and social networks.

Keeley and Clarke (2002) conducted a quantitative study for the Princess Royal Trust with a representative sample of 3800 carers, 400 professionals and decision makers. They asked about many issues including carer's experiences of the CA. They found that 25% of carers had had a CA, a downward trend from 38% in 1998. The low level of CA was similar to that recorded by councils in England through the Social Services Performance Assessment Framework Indicators where the average was 21% with variation from 10% in London to 25% in the Shire councils.

Glendinning (2011) observed that most European Union carers are co-resident with the cared-for, which is consistent with UK data. Carers may be wary of CA, fearing that assessment might lead to institutional care of the person being supported, (Arksey and Glendinning 2007). Research by Jorgenson et al (2009) used a qualitative approach with telephone interviews of 300 carers. They concluded that carers are a vulnerable group which is undervalued, under rated and underprovided for. Their research showed that there is a contradiction between policy and practice which was also observed by Power (2008). Carers UK (2005) asked 1,207 carers about their experience of dealing with emergency. The results make the current research relevant as follow up on how service provision impacts carers' lives. The carers' quotes from the Carers UK (2005) findings reveal statements of concern;

I was left to sort it myself.

I was told there are no services.

A qualitative study by Beresford et al (2005) proved that services were frequently thought to be 'out of synch with people's lifestyles' and statements from carers and service users in that research endorsed this;

Life changes and increased disablement are hard enough, to access care you have to do the donkey work whilst coming to terms with major life changes.

Although the study by Wales and Pryjmachuk (2009) was based on mental health carers, it has important overall implications on carers. Despite having a legal right to assessment, only a minority has had a CA, (Wales & Pryjmachuk 2009) and they found confusion over the definition of 'carer'. Scourfield (2005) stated that the word 'carer' has been socially constructed in such a way that many people who look after the vulnerable or dependent-others do not identify themselves. Wales & Pryjmachuk (2009) recommended that practice could be improved by clarifying the definition of 'carer', redesigning the CA form and offering wider choice of evidence based services; dovetailing service user and carer needs assessment and active support and engagement of carers.

2.3 Literature gap

Most of the research on carers used qualitative research design with in-depth face to face interviews to capture the carers' story. People with LD have higher incidence of mental health problems (Barr et al, 1999) and the fact that they are living longer means that the caring role has been extended. This highlights the importance of CA and support services for carers and the need to find out how services impact lives. The Princess Royal Trust for Carers (2002) proved that many care for 20-50 hours a week or more. This makes the current research valuable in providing carer perceptions of assessment and the impact of service provision on caring.

Despite the increasing number of studies and policies related to improving supports for carers, recent studies on caring (Yeandle et al, 2007; Montgomery, 2011; Carers UK, 2009) still indicate high stress levels among carers, adverse physical and emotional health, and carers living in poverty. Therefore, there seems to a mismatch between policy, service delivery and how service is received. A systematic review of 29 studies on the effects of respite care on carers' well-being recommended a more 'carer-centred' approach to provision of services, (McNally et al, 1999). Carers' saving of the UK government revenue has an upward trend from £87 billion a year (Buckner and Yeandle, 2007) to £119 (Buckner and Yeandle, 2011) by providing care free of charge. The cost savings of the service carers offer make research on the impact of services policy offers to carers by a CA an important area of research.

The identified gap in literature exists due to the increased life expectancy for people with LD (Cuskelly 2006) making caring a life time work; and the welfare of people with LD depends on the sustained physical, mental social and economic wellbeing of carers (Burton-Smith et al 2006). Very little is known on the extended caring role and this highlights a gap in the existing literature. That makes the impact of services received after a CA important focus for research to inform policy and service delivery (Parmenter 2004). No study has examined the direct perceptions of the assessment experiences of carers of people with LD who have had their needs assessed; and what the impact of service accessed is on the carer and caring. This study seeks to address this gap in the literature on care giving.

Chapter 3   RESEARCH DESIGN AND METHODOLOGY

3.1 Introduction

This chapter describes the research methodology in detail and justification for the design choice. It explains the procedures followed in research, sampling, the sample, the tools used in the research and the problems faced in data collection.

3.2 Research design

A Qualitative approach employed in this study as qualitative research methods attempt to tap the deeper meanings of particular human experiences (Rubin, 2008) and are interested in life as it is lived in real situations, (Woods, 2006). Therefore, qualitative approach is best suited for this study as it 'lift veils' (Blumer, 1976) to explore carers' experiences and the meanings in 'thick description', (Denzin, 1989) of their perceptions of the CA process and of the impact of services they opted for or not. A quantitative approach would be unable to gather such detail. In addition, Qualitative research design was used because little is known about the experience of having a CA, experiences and impact of receiving services for carers of people with LD; for this reason, a qualitative approach is best; and for this reason, the best examples of this phenomenon (Morse, 2006) are the carers who have been assessed and are in receipt of services.

Savenye and Robinson (2005), define qualitative research as devoted to developing an understanding of human systems. Atkinson et al (1998) allude that most qualitative approaches focus on natural settings; have an interest in meanings, perspectives and understandings. The 'thick description' this study collected reflected history into CA and service access experience, the carers' voices, feelings, actions and meanings, (Denzin, 1989). To collect this kind of data, the researcher should have empathy to win the confidence of participants and create a rapport which allows the participants to talk about their experiences, Denzin (1989). Qualitative research allowed the researcher to be open to 'multiple realities,' (Savenye and Robinson, 2005) of the CA experience and receiving service because the researcher wants to know what is happening, (Savenye and Robinson, 2005). The researcher extracted meaning from the experiences which are able to generate themes from the patterns that emerged. Strauss (1990) calls this grounded research, as there is closeness of fit between theory and data, (Woods, 2006).

3.3 Research Methodology

Burton (2006) says that it is impossible for social care professionals to conduct social care research without prior knowledge of the area of study. It is important for the reader to understand that the author of this study is a carer who has also worked as a paid carer in many social care settings. Many scholars (Miller, 2001; Collins & Green, 1990) believe that researchers should be members of the same group they study in order to have subjective knowledge necessary to truly understand the life experience although Taylor et al (1995) says an outsider may elicit explanations that are assumed to be known to someone with insider status. Riesman (1993) talks about fractures in qualitative design where the interviewee responds to the researcher based on who the researcher is, age, gender, class, race and whether the researcher is a member of their group and when the researcher does not share in their group a social distance is created which can affect the data collected. In this research this was reduced by the fact that the researcher was a staff member of CC where carers where recruited from. It was not difficult to create trust and rapport as the staff at CC had already built this over 20 years and it was easier for the researcher to fit into what the staff had already achieved. Glassner and Loughlin (1987) believe that social distance can be reduced by establishing trust, showing genuine interest, assuring confidentiality and not being judgmental which helps participants to feel comfortable and competent enough to talk back (Blumer, 1969), to point out misinterpretations and offer corrections.

Although qualitative design is criticised for not being generalizable, as in this research the participants were 10, Woods (2006) says there are two ways in which it is generalisable; through the theory that is generated and through its contribution to an archive of studies on a particular issue which then can be reinterpreted. Woods (2006) warns that immersion in qualitative study can lead to either 'going native' and 'macro blindness', or both, making the researcher oblivious to outside forces operating on the situation. The researcher worked together with staff at the CC to design the research instrument in order to avoid this. Therefore, a Qualitative approach was deemed as the most suitable for this study.

Reliability is the relative absence of errors of measurement in a measuring tool (Mark, 1996). Validity is the extent to which an empirical measure adequately reflects the real meaning of the concept under consideration, (Rubin and Babbie, 2008). The reliability, validity, internal consistency and trustworthiness of this research stem from the use of the same questions with each participant using a clear, ambiguity free semi-structured interview schedule designed with help from staff at CC who have had more experience working with carers; the naturalness of the discussions with each participant which brought out the issues when the researcher elicited full honest and open responses without undue influence; and sufficient time given to each participant to talk at length whilst the researcher recorded key points. Qualitative researchers can achieve validity by rigorous subjectivity (Wolcott, 1994). Woods (2006) argues that validity or rigour in qualitative research depends on: the researcher taking unobtrusive measures; respondent validation by giving the researcher's understanding of the participant's meaning back to them to judge. Being a carer, the researcher had to bracket, (Ashworth, 1996), herself to set aside researcher assumptions about the experiences of caring and make the research about the carer's experiences and this added to trustworthiness.

3.4 The Sample and Piloting

In order to recruit carers for the study, the researcher attended Carers' meetings to present the study, giving carers the information sheet. This allowed carers to ask questions about the study and make an informed choice as to participate or not. Participation in the study was on a voluntary basis. Carers were assured of confidentiality and their right to withdraw any time from the study without giving any reason. The researcher contacted those carers who met the criteria for the research, i.e. looking after a person with LD, had CA and indicated willingness to participate in the recorded interview. The interviews took place in a location of their choice.

A purposive sampling approach was used to recruit carers for this study. Purposive sampling is key informant survey which targets individuals who are knowledgeable about the issue under investigation, (Engel and Schutt, 2009). Rubin and Rubin (1995) purport that participants must be knowledgeable, willing to talk and represent a range of points of view. This type of sampling is known as non random and non probability sampling since the researcher's purpose is not to generalise but to get an understanding, (Woods, 2006) of the CA experiences of carers and of the impact of CA and service access to enhance knowledge about processes and events. Purposive or judgmental sampling was ideal to select the 10 carers who fit in the scope of study. According to Fuller and Petch (1995) all instruments designed by the researcher must be piloted before they are used for the main study as this ensures that it works, produces valid and reliable data required for the study. The researcher conducted a pilot study with 3 carers. This allowed the testing of the interview questions, to ensure that they were understandable and asked in the correct order. The questions were not adjusted as the 3 carers understood what was being asked. The interview allowed carers to talk about their experiences in a setting where confidentiality was assured, ensuring researcher sensitivity to talk about potentially distressing issues. The face-to-face interview allowed for unanticipated explanations to emerge and to be explored with participants talking about their experiences in their own way. The interview guide ensured that the same areas were covered in each interview, (Matthews and Ross 2010).

Table 1, (on the next page) summarizes the characteristics of the participants in the study. The interviews lasted between 35 to 55 minutes long and they were hand recorded. The recording took place immediately after the interviews from the notes made during the interview so as not to disrupt the interview conversation flow. The recordings and transcriptions were kept in a secure place. The total (N=10) was made up of 2 male carers and 8 female carers. The sample consisted of British, European, African, Caribbean and South America participants. Most of the carers are parent carers (N= 8) of whom 3 were older parent carers. Two participants are kinship carers for siblings. The carers' age ranged from 29 to 71. 4 participants, 2 females and 2 males, had retired. Of these, the two female and 1 male, were parents caring for adult children with learning disabilities. The average age of the participants was 55.3 years. Of the cared-for, 7 were male and 3 females, and their age ranged from 7 to 74 years, with one cared-for in retirement age otherwise the other 9 age ranged from 7 to 42 years. The average age of the cared-for was 28.5years. There was diversity in LD with 2 affected by Down syndrome, 7 on the autism spectrum and one with Cornelia de Lang Syndrome.

Table1.

Participants   Carer age gender and ethnicity, Cared for relationship to carer, age, gender and ethnicity   LD and complexities

1   57, Female, White British of Portuguese origin   Son, 24, Male, British   LD, Little speech, inactive

2   71, Female, Black British of Caribbean origin   Son, 38, Male, British   LD, challenging behavior

3   67, Female, White British.   Son, 23, Male, British   Autism, mild LD, Obesity, challenging behavior

4   40, Female, White British of Greek Cypriot origin   Son, 16, Male, British   Cornelia de Lang Syndrome, Stays in dark room, Challenging behavior, little speech

5   71, Male, White British of Italian origin Sister, 74, Female   Down syndrome, moderate LD, Poor sight, diabetes, slower mobility, more forgetful

6   29, Female, Black British of African origin   Son, 7, Male   Autism, Severe LD, Severe challenges, spitting, biting, smearing faeces, ADHD

7   56, Female, Black British of African origin   Daughter, 27, Female. Moderate LD, Epileptic, left side paralysis

8   41, Female, White British of Turkish origin   Son, 11, Male   Autism, severe LD, Challenging behavior, low attention span

9   71, Male, White British of Polish origin Son, 39, Male   LD, Poor mobility is in wheelchair, hard of hearing

| 10 | 50, Female, Black British of British Guyana origin | Sister, 42, Female down syndrome, stuttered speech |

3.5 Research ethics

Research ethics consider the interaction between researchers and the people they study (Woods 2006) ensuring that researchers consider the needs and concerns of the participants and establish trust. Ethical criteria for research are; autonomy which includes informed consent, privacy, anonymity and confidentiality; non-malevolence; beneficence; justice and positive contribution of knowledge (Beauchamp 1982) and respect for communities Woods (2006). This study adhered to the Social Work professional body, HCPC's code of ethics which are governed by the National Association of Social Workers codes of ethics (1994) which includes anti-oppressive practice and working without disempowering the research participants. This study ensured that research participant's detailed information does not appear in the dissertation or any report which can identify them. Any quotes used do not contain research participant identification information. A telephone number to access counselling was provided the participants in case they become distressed. Participants were free to withdraw from the interview at any point. The ethics clearance involved approaching management at the Carers Centre and the University Ethics Board.

Capacity issues were considered very carefully. Advice was sought from expert colleagues at the CC as well as from other sources. The Mental Capacity Act, 2007, in particular the General Principles contained in the Act together with other guidance enabled the researcher to develop clear guidance about asking for consent. Carers were asked for their consent to record the interviews.

3.6 Confidentiality, informed consent, voluntary participation.

Informed consent is one of the most important tools for ensuring respect for participants, (Woods, 2006). The information sheet, (Appendix C) described the research and the participants signed the consent form (Appendix B) to document their consent to participate, (Woods, 2006). The researcher explained to management of the Carer Centre (CC) and to each potential participant: the purpose of the research; what is expected of a research participant; expected risks and benefits, including psychological and social; the fact voluntary participation is voluntary and withdrawal with no negative repercussions; confidentiality protection; information of the research supervisor to be contacted for questions or problems related to the research, (Woods, 2006).

3.7 The Instrument

Two research tools were used in this study, the researcher and the semi-structured interview guide. The researcher, as a tool for carrying out the interview, had to be skilled at the interview task and have self-detachment

(Gillham, 2005). The researcher needed to be flexible and adaptable to different participants whilst ensuring that the same topics are discussed in an atmosphere conducive for the participant to give their answers (Matthews and Ross, 2010).

This study used a semi-structured interview schedule on all participants in face-to-face interviews. The research relied on noting down key points during the interview and then typing the notes soon afterwards. Although Bernard (1988) stresses that memory should not be relied on and tape recorders should be used to record exact words as this is crucial later in analysis and report writing; the participant choice not to be tape recorded, which took precedence, made note taking a necessity in this research. Eight carers were interviewed at the CC and two in their own home.

The data gathered included demographic data for carer's age, gender and country of origin. Questions for the carers focused on the assessment experience and the impact of services accessed. Data, age and relationship to the carer, other health problems, were gathered about the cared-for but they were not interviewed. The semi-structured interview guide was designed from a literature review to explore the carers' experiences. The interview guide incorporated open questions, where the researcher had a fair idea of what is going on with the phenomenon but not enough to predict the answer, (Richards and Morse, 2007). The use of closed-ended questions would have been disempowering to carers as the questions can marginalise perspectives by imposition of preconceived and inflexible options. This problem was minimised through the use of open-ended questions which can evoke explanatory responses. The probes for each question depended on participant responses and they ensured exploration of the research phenomenon, (Matthews and Ross, 2010). In the interviews, the researcher used conversational techniques such as checking on apparent contradictions, asking for clarification and playing devil's advocate, (Woods, 2006) to gain participant perspectives.

The interview guide, (Appendix A), had an introduction which allowed explanations about the research, confidentiality, signing consent form and collecting bio-demographical data. The interview guide ending ensured the participant was not distressed. The interview schedule was used in order to answer the 3 broad questions of this research. The questions were structured to capture the participant's experiences of social care services and the carer's perceived impact. The researcher was a skilled facilitator for the interviews, actively listening, recording key points, non verbal signs and keeping the participant focused on the subject whilst exploring major themes brought up by each participant.

The researcher participated in active interview, as described by Holstein and Gubrium, (2003) which they described as an interpersonal drama with a developing plot. The researcher paid attention to the process and product so that the interview generated socially constructed knowledge (Holstein and Gubrium, 2003) and became a meaning-making conversation which is interactional and constructive (Holstein and Gubrium, 2003) and reality was continually under construction (Garfinkel, 1967). The interviews encouraged participants to develop the topic in a way that is relevant to the carer's experiences, (DeVault, 1990). Silverman (2001) believes that it is in the interactive components of interviewing without controlling and reducing the interview that deep mutual understanding, which is used to build knowledge and social worlds, is achieved. Good data collection is the basis for quotations to be selected for later inclusion (Thomson et al, 2002). The interview allows recording of non-verbal signal and spontaneous reactions (Payne &Payne 2006) which are a source of information.

The notes taken during the interviews were typed within one hour of the interview into verbatim written format on the long train journey back home by the researcher. Rawlings (1988) says that careful transcription and coding is important for drawing conclusions. The typed transcripts were identified by participant code number. Names were removed for confidentiality and replaced with a number, interview location, date and time of interview.

3.8 Data analysis

In qualitative research, data collection and analysis are intertwined (Janesick, 1998) and analysis begins almost immediately, (Woods, 2006). This research approach generated a lot of statements as data about carers' experiences, many view points, both negative and positive, which were used to answer the research questions.

This research used thematic data analysis as guided by Miles and Huberman (1994), which focuses on identifiable themes and patterns of living or behavior, (Aronson, 1992). It is a process of segmentation, categorising and rethinking aspects of the data prior to final interpretation (Grbich, 2007). Themes are recurrent statements about a subject of inquiry (Boyatzis, 1998) or fundamental concepts that characterise specific experiences of individuals, (Ryan and Bernard, 2003). Themes are developed from codes. Codes are efficient data-labelling and data retrieval devices which empower and speed up analysis, Miles and Huberman (1994). Miles and Huberman (1994) recommend naming codes using a name closest to the concept. The codes were created from concepts in the data so that the code structure reflected the ground, i.e., the experiences of the participants, (Bradley et al, 2007), interpreting accounts of participants to get the meaning and looking for relationship between different parts of data to explain differences and relationships, (Mathews and Ross (2010) and returning to the research questions to see if the analysis answered them.

The printed and stored transcriptions were analysed and re-analysed. The researcher went over the 10 transcriptions to identify parts forming a pattern which were highlighted in different colours and coded, (Appendix G). The researcher identified 19 codes, (Table A , in Appendix H) as part of data reduction, which Miles and Huberman (1994) describe as a process of selecting, focusing, simplifying, abstracting and transforming data to elicit meaning. The codes with an interrelated pattern formed 14 sub-themes. These were grouped together around a central concept, which became the major themes, as shown in the data threading (b) on Appendix H. Developing codes is a lengthy process but Miles and Huberman (1994) allude that well-crafted, clear and comprehensive code structure promotes the quality of analysis. The codes were finalized at the point of theoretical saturation, the point at which no new concepts emerge, (Patton, 2002). The researcher identified this point of saturation after analysing and re-analysing all the transcripts. Charmaz (1995) says that coding, categorising participants' stories results in having only parts of the story and not the whole and this fractures qualitative design.

Analysis of data was made easier by displaying data visually using tables to show the results of the themes. Miles and Huberman (1994), hold that data display is a critical and often underutilized means of analysis. They note that increasingly, qualitative research involves analyzing what they call within-case data from individuals and cross-case data, from many participants. The researcher identified 5 major themes, (Table 2 page 46): Telling their story, Self development, Life on hold: Coping strategies and Formal Services. 14 sub-themes were identified, respite, worry with community access, care sharing, religion, carer's health, multi role of the carer, challenging behaviour, leisure, work, education, short courses, the assessment process, the impact of assessment and the experience of having a CA.

Miles and Huberman (1994) describe the last type of data analysis activity as drawing and verifying conclusions. The researcher set out to write the analysis using theory to back up the findings and checking the original objectives to see if they had been achieved.

3.9 Problems encountered in data collection

The researcher made several presentations about the research to carers. There were carers who were willing to participate but most did not have a CA. A major challenge was in identifying carers who met the inclusion criteria; carers of people with LD who had CA; and were willing to participate in a recorded interview. So, although the research initially aimed to pilot 3 participants and interview 15 making a total of 18, it was difficult to achieve that. The researcher was able to identify 7 more participants after the pilot study to give a complement of 10. LoBiondo-Wood & Haber (1998) argue that results collected from under ten participants tend to be unstable. It is possible that the researcher listening and writing down key points during the interviews might have interfered with responding sensitively or led to loss of data. The researcher typed the whole conversation from key points noted within one hour of the interview on the 1.5 hour journey back home. In paraphrasing after the interview, it is possible that some data could have been lost and the researcher may have imposed her own linguistic structures and ideas on the words of the participants. It is possible that the researcher taking notes of key points during the interview might have influenced the participant during the interview.

Chapter 4   FINDINGS, ANALYSIS AND DISCUSSION

4.0.0 Introduction

This chapter discusses the findings which are tabulated in the Appendices. The chapter analyses each sub-theme identified in the light of theory and evidence-based research. It discusses the link of the major themes to the research question to decide if the research purpose has been achieved.

4.0.1 Results

Table 2 below shows the five major themes (in bold print) and 14 sub-themes identified in the research.   The other tables of results are at the back of the book.

Table 2 Themes

Telling their story: assessment process; assessment experience and assessment impact.

Self-development: Leisure; Work; Education and Short courses.

Life on hold: Carer's health; Multi role of the carer and challenging behaviour.

Coping Strategies: Care sharing and Religion.

Formal Services: Respite; Worry with community access.

Most of the questions elicited long sequence of response which lead to issues related to the caring role, the cared-for and policy, which became the focus of the sub-themes.

Telling their story

4.0.2 Assessment Process

As shown in Table 3, all 10 participants were assessed by social workers in their homes between 2005 and 2009. The social workers remained actively involved after the CA with participants 6 and participant 8. Each of the ten participants was referred to the Carers Centre (CC) as shown by participant 4;

teachers ....talked about an assessment of my needs. The head teacher called social services, an appointment was made....The social worker came to my house

4.0.3 Assessment experience

The findings, in Table 4, show that participants 2 and 3 talked about raised expectations which were not met. The assessment process was an experience enjoyed by all, as summed up by participant 7:

It was lovely actually. Oh I talked and talked...social worker was very patient and listened to me going on and on.. I felt good afterwards.

4.0.4 Assessment impact

Table 5 shows that six participants, (5, 6, 4, 8, 9 and 10) had positive experience from the referral to social network at the CC. Five participants did not hear from social services after the CA. Four participants, 1, 2 , 3 and 7) were already using the CC before the CA so social worker referral to the CC through the assessment did not make a difference in their lives. So although the leisure and social networking from the CC impacted positively on the participants, the overall perception was that the services from CA did not meet participants' needs. Participant 4;

respite .. care plan was made.... I ... made.. friends among the carers ... My life has a bit more quality to it...

Self Development

4.0.5   Leisure

Table 6 shows that nine participants use the leisure activities at the CC and one participant, participant 1, does not have enough time because of two other young children whose needs place more demands on her time. Participant 6 uses leisure time to sleep.

4.0.6   Education

Table 7 findings show that nine participants did not use the education service. There are two main reasons for not taking education. Participant 10 was the only one of the 10 to take education.

4.0.7   Short courses

Table 8 indicates that all ten participants took park in short courses run by the CC although some don't have much time, as shown by participant 2;

I have followed up ..courses for flower arrangement, pottery, baking etc .. budgets, benefits, art, craft, managing various conditions like diabetes, challenging behavior

4.0.8　　　Work

Table 9 shows that participants 3 and 9 work as retired volunteers. Participants 8 and 10 are in paid part-time employment. Participant 10 took over the caring role from her mother and at that time stopped working but as a result of the CA, she was able to resume work. Six participants, five women (one is retired) and one man who was retired, were not working.

Life on hold

4.0.9　　　Carers health

Table 10 shows that participants 3, 7, 8, 10 and 9 did not discuss their health. Participants 1, 2, 4, 5, and 6 mentioned health related issues, summed up by participant 1;

the extra support .. on my arm and hand. I have shoulder problems ..had..two operations on the shoulder. ...painful joints and high blood pressure.

4.1.0　　　Multi role of the carer

In Table 11, the retired female carer, participant 3, raised cross-generational issues in her role as grandmother. Participants 1 and 3 raised issues relating to the name 'carer' being out of context with their many roles. All that participants are busy with many different aspects of their lives as shown by participant 10;

I .. transport my mum and sister around..... I work ... for half a day four times a week and ..　　do my assignments..

4.1.1 Challenging behaviour

In Table 12, seven participants, 1, 2, 3, 4, 5, 6 and 8, highlighted the issues relating to challenging behaviour. Participants 2 and 4 discussed issues of mental health problems affecting the cared-for. Participant 4:

... he.. sitting in the dark.. curtains are dark. …. when he is not ready to let you into his world,… becomes challenging, breaking things.

Coping Strategies
4.1.2 Care Sharing

Table 13 shows that eight participants care share. Participant 1, 6, 7, 8 are lone carers whose relationships broke down. Participants 10, 9, 2 and 5 are lone carers because of death or illness of the primary carer. Participant 7;

my four other children help me … all work and live in different parts of the city. My ex husband does not help

4.1.3 Religion

Table 14 shows 8 out of 10 participants value their faith personally and for social networking. The cared-for enjoy religious gatherings. All 8 participants said this topic was not discussed in the Carer's Assessment. Participant 1;

My faith carries me through difficult times…. No, the topic did not come up during the assessment.

Formal Services

4.1.4 Respite

In Table 15, only 3 participants have used the Local Authority respite, although one of them, participant 3 stopped later. 6 participants would rather have family take care of the cared-for to get real respite. Participant 4;

Our families look after him ..we take a break. ..they all know him ..and how to deal with challenging behavior. He ...enjoys the attention...

4.1.5 Worry with community Access

Table 16 shows the issues raised about community access for people with LD. Participant 3 raised issues of spending cuts and employment, community banter and worry with independent living. Participants 2 and 3 mentioned the dietary impact of community access, obesity and weight loss. People with LD also limit their own access as shown by participant 7 whose views are shared by participants 10, 9. People cared-for by participants 1 and 5 access the community without any issues of concern. Participant 7;

I tried to engage her in activities in the community but she was unwilling to do them and she does not like crowds.

Discussion

Telling their story

4.2.0 Assessment Process

Each participant was referred to the Carer's Centre (CC) after the Carer's Assessment (CA) (although 4 had already been using the CC before the CA). When the needs of the carer and cared-for met certain criteria, social workers stayed on the case after referral as shown by participant 6 and 8 who have young children which challenging behavior. This finding agrees with the results of Carers UK (2007) study which proved that support services increased were vulnerability was identified.

The results show that the process of Carers Assessment was working according to policy guide lines which require collaboration by different agencies; GPs (participant 6), schools (participant 1) which identify carers and make referrals. This is summed up by participant 2;

CC..... staff made a referral.. a social worker visited .... hopes were raised ... to be assessed and not receive any feedback, it's not nice.

It was easier in sampling to find carers of people with learning disabilities but difficult to find carers of people with learning disabilities who had had a CA; showing that more carers still have to be assessed but most had been referred to the CC. There was no follow up from practitioners for five participants after the CA. It looks like participants had high expectations which were not met when there was no feedback and follow-up from social services and this does not speak well of partnership. Middleton (1997) states that assessment is a basis for decision about whether and how to intervene after information gathering on feasibility of effecting change and should not just be a form filling exercise for filing. Practitioners did CA and to effect change, the CC was the next stage in intervention but the participants felt the process was incomplete.

4.2.1 Assessment experience

The data indicated that the participants perceived the assessment process as social service's reach to them as partners and it was an enjoyable chance to talk about themselves. Participant 8 sums up the general feel of all the participants;

It was lovely actually, I must have talked for England... about my caring and how it affects me. She filled in a form.

4.2.2 Assessment impact

Government approach on carers (Twiggs & Atkins 1994) separates the carer from the cared-for by providing assistance for the cared-for in the form of personal budget or direct payments. This is what allows carers to take a break and access leisure, work, respite and education. Participant 2 sums this up;

my assessment and his reassessment for his benefits ... gave us a personal assistant.... indirectly I benefit from time to myself.

Both sibling participants reported positive impact from the CA. The sibling sister, participant 10 is caring for her sister, her frail mother, a double caring role and working at the same time. Other carers with double caring role are participants 6 and 10, looking after an ailing parent; participants 1, 6 and 8 have young children. Rose et al (2009) highlighted the stress of Sandwiched care giving, between caring for the needs of the young children, the disabled and the needs of elderly parents. Such added responsibility emphasises the need for communication and partnership, amongst families, multi-disciplinary service providers and flexibility from employers. Where social workers saw vulnerability, they worked with the multiagency to manage challenging behaviour with participant 6 and 8 who had young children with LD who displayed challenging behaviour. Participants 5 (the elderly participant) and 10, who has a double caring role were referred only to the CC. Participant 6 proves this;

Almost immediately after my assessment .... I got time to distress.....

All participants indicated positive impact from the activities of the CC. 6 participants felt that the CA, overall had no impact on their caring, four of these had already been benefitting from the services of the CC before their CA. These results are almost similar with the findings of the Manchester City CA survey of 2009 which showed that of the sample of 587 participants, 175 participants had big positive impact, 210 had small difference and 125 had no impact from the CA. The 2 sibling participants had a CA almost at the same time they took over the primary carer role at a stressful time, so the impact of the CA was immediately positive.

Participant 10 was the only participant who made use of all the services on offer, education, work, respite and leisure. Research by SCIE would suggest that policy and practice are not meeting the three levels of co-production: Compliance; recognition and support ; and transformation. Carers should be 'co-producers', (Chung and Schneider, 2002), in the services that involve them; and Seddon et al (2006) recommended the need for practitioners to engage carers as partners. There was no input from carers on the choice of services available after a CA so the participants comply selectively with the services which they had no hand in choosing. To be empowered a person requires an environment that provides options and ascribes authority to the person to choose, (Rapp and Goscha, 2006). Services are being cut. The CC where this research was carried out lost funding and closed in mid 2012, this is not supporting carers. The CC for most carers is often the only place carers can talk about issues affecting them freely with staff and other carers. What replaces the services being cut should provide quality services not a business oriented environment which shuts carers out. Change cannot take place in carers' lives if they are not empowered to partner with practitioners to suggest services they want, to be consulted when services are being cut and also about the services which replace them, to get feedback and ongoing checkup after CA so the process becomes cyclical. Social work operates on personal, cultural and structural power in which the social worker has power and works with people who have been affected by power, (Thompson 2006). Effective communication, which gives and receives feedback in CA, should empower carers to approach practitioners to make their expectations from a CA known as practitioners are aware that, 'power and powerlessness corrupt,' (Wardhaugh and Wilding, 1993). The CA should not have been an end itself but the beginning of a co-production partnership process. The Kinship Care Alliance has designed a form for CA which was being piloted in 12 Local Authorities aimed to improve co-production partnership by encouraging collaboration between social workers and carers and to open working partnership which draws on the family's strengths.

Self Development

4.2.3   Leisure

Four participants had been using the CC for leisure before their CA. Accounts of all participants indicated that social networking arranged by the CC had a positive effect on them. This finding agrees with research by Wilkie and Barr (2008) that carers want increased leisure activities; and that CC provide short breaks for a few hours (MacDonald & Callery 2004). Participant 10 summed up;

I come to the CC for relaxation and meeting other carers ...I enjoy the trips.. learn new things. ...I come back home a better carer.

Wiggs & Stores (1996) found that more than half of the participants in their research with families whose child with LD had sleep disturbance had not received treatment. The study by Doo & Wing (2006) investigated sleep problems in Chinese children with LD and the relationship to parental stress using a questionnaire with 210 parents. They concluded that parents of children with sleep problems experienced higher levels of stress and need early management of the problems. Participant 6 illustrated this and stressed the irrelevance of most of the services that come with a CA. She uses short respite/leisure time to sleep showing that if the child is on treatment, it is not yet working;

..my son goes .. special school ... daughter goes .. different school. I .. sleep during .. the day because my son sleeps 4 hours in the night.

Time is limited for participant 1;

I take (children) to school,..come back to deal with ......'s self care. ...... if I get 10 minutes ...with a cup of tea, that's leisure.

Deimling (1992) observed that for many carers, a large block of free time is still not enough to help them access leisure because 'mental freedom' from caring is a critical element of accessing leisure regardless of how much respite time is available as they are caring mentally and cannot relax. This implies a rethinking of fresh approaches to reduce mental caring in the government approach on separating the carer from the cared for (Twigg and Atkins 1994) using short breaks.

4.2.4   Education

The results show that nine participants did not take up education, as in long formal courses. The main reason proves the burden of caring, shared by 3 other participants and summed up by participant 1 is;

..that is not relevant to my life .. now. ,.... as there are no hours (in the day for me to do that)

Views of participant 6 and 3 are shared by participant 4;

....because they always call me at his college ... if there are behavior problems.

This has implications on whether the Care Plan is capturing all the issues if paid trained staff from the different service providers are unable to cope or feel that they are limited by accountability and therefore resort to stopping the carer from getting a much earned short break. It also implies that there is expertise that carers of people with learning disabilities have acquired which society is not benefiting from through training. Practitioners are challenged by the New Care Act, 2014, to enhance wellbeing for the carer though robust care planning. Participant 10 was the only one to take education and fit the nature of the education to caring role by home studying;

I have done a teaching assistant course and have just completed it.

... applied for an educational grant.. I enrolled for the home training course...

Research by Green Lister (2003) on Lifelong Learning concluded there are barriers to education faced by one excluded group, mature women carers. It is worth noting that, in this dissertation, the main insights into LD issues were brought forward by mature men and women, participants, 1, 2, 3, 5, 7 and 9 They are very insightful and aware of implications of policy on practical life. True partnership should be able to harness the life lessons this age group has to offer so that education is about carers teaching the knowledge they gained as well as learning what they like. Gabanillas in Roodin (2011) defines intergenerational learning as 'educational exchanges between generations' and calls for the expertise in the mature people across all cultures to participate in knowledge transfer and transform society.

4.2.5 Short courses

All 10 participants took park in short courses, diabetes, flower arrangement etc run by the CC although some don't have much time. Their views are represented by participant 4;

I have done short two hour courses ... Those are relevant to my life and fit in the short amount of time I have.

Hayman (2005) used the Carers' Education Exchange Program to teach carers. Although it was used for carers of those with a mental illness, its use indicated how this can reduce isolation, develop skills relevant to the caring role, the formation of supportive networks and promote self-care and a positive outlook.

4.2.6 Work

Four participants work, part time although two are retired volunteers. This finding agrees with the research by Johnson and Lo Sasso (2006) which concluded that care provision significantly reduces the hours worked. Arksey and Glendinning (2007), arrived at the same conclusion in their qualitative study, with 80 carers in England, finding that most carers opt for part time work and therefore lower wages. Separation of the carer from the cared-for using a personal budget, the Equality law and the availability of formal support services such as school, help to keep participants in work. Research by Carmichael et al (2008) confirmed that carers continue to face difficulties of combining employment and care in spite of recent policy initiatives designed to help them. Participant 3 captures the issues which have negative implications on the Care Plans;

… always called .. his college ….. the care plan does not capture some of the nuances of the challenges faced by carers …. carers have inbuilt risk assessment procedures, but public does not.

It is a challenge for practitioners to work closely with families to make effective fit-for purpose care plans to meet the Care Act 2014 economic well-being for carers. Carers have gained expertise and knowledge which is not being used for society's gain. The other 6 participants, 5 women and 1 retired male, do not work, agreeing with what research has shown that carers are more likely to be female in the UK (Arksey & Hirst, 2005; Lazaro et al 2004).

Life on hold

4.2.7   Carers health

Five participants did not raise health issues. Participants 1, 2, 4, 5, and 6 experienced worry and concern for their poor health agreeing with the research by Cheung (2004) and Carers UK (2005) that carers have their own health problems. Participant 2 sums it up;

It (caring) is a lot of work which requires me to be alert all the time.

Retired sibling participant 5 who is looking after his older sibling;

I have use of one arm because of polio and my joints are now a problem….

Participant 4 put her own life on hold, risking her health by slotting her operation at a more convenient time around caring;

I even had my operation on a Thursday. .. The doctor said I shouldn't do any work. Who would do it, I ask? ... (laughs).. I ended up going back into hospital ...

Al-Janabi et al (2011) recommended that considering outcomes for a sole carer may understate the degree of spillover effect any intervention may have on the multiple carers involved in care sharing. Participant 4 laughed and her observable gestures indicated that there was little or no other support and therefore her going back into hospital meant that care spilled over to informal support. The current CA form had information about an emergency plan as policy's response to research done by Beresford (1995) which showed that there was no emergency plan. Nottinghamshire County Council was using a five stage CA plan to meet changing needs and co-production policy. It may be worth taking this nationally to ensure that practitioners and policy makers have knowledge and understanding of the factors that complicate coping, (Kuupelomaki et al 2004). The Care Act of 2014 gives all carers the right to an Assessment of their needs and they do not have to be providing substantial care on a regular basis. The Act has a 'well-being principle' which requires assessment of how caring impact on carer well-being and what outcomes the carers wish for.

4.2.8 Multi role of the carer

Findings indicate that all participants lead busy lives, agreeing with research by Deimling (1992). They fit everything around caring as summed up by participant 5;

I attend activities at the CC ... I also have ... indoor games at... Centre and dancing at ... I belong to a walking club...

The researcher could not find current evidence-based research on how grandparents pass on the sensitivity of LD to the grand children in order to cope with cross-generational caring. Participant 3 raised these issues in her role as grandmother;

... ...His siblings' children help him as well, so that LD .... is being sensitised to the next generation......

As a grandmother, she established meaningful intergenerational relationships to maintain loving, enduring and sustainable relationships that positively accommodate her multi roles. This is an untapped skill which is empowering the next generation to develop care abilities in generations that catch, not learn, caring in the interstitial world of watching and being involved in family care activities whilst growing up. Such generations can only impact society positively in whatever they do. The Manchester City CA survey (2009) advocated a whole family approach which has been adapted by Children's Society, Disabled Parents Network, Princess Royal Trust for Carers Network and by the Care Act 2014. They observed that young carers do not care in isolation from the rest of the family. Although participant 3's grandchildren are not primary carers, the participant is fulfilling her grand parenting role of providing support for grand children to understand LD issues for the welfare of the whole family. The Care Act of 2014 whole family approach to the Carers Assessment should capture the support network available to the carer and cared-for. Ahuja & Williams (2005) argue that carers are a potentially, underutilized teaching resource with expertise defined by experience which brings perspectives and ways of thinking that can instill a new dimension to delivering care services and training; and that blending this expertise with that of professionals can bring best outcomes. It is a challenge for policy makers, trainers, practitioners and service providers to make use of knowledge and skills which carers have acquired for the betterment of service provision.

The data suggested that there are issues relating to the name 'carer' as raised by participants 1 and 3. This finding is similar to the research by Wales and Prymachuk (2009) who recommended clarification of the definition. Labelling people is disempowering, (Concannon, 2005) because 'language is... a system of communication but also a vehicle of power,' (Gergen, 1999) as the terms of defining people maintain societal power dynamics leaving groups oppressed. Through policy, practitioners can challenge the use of this word which the named group does not identify with. This is taking up arms against structural oppression, (Wilson et al 2008).   Participant 1;

... carer, means they are... forgetting about my other relationships …. I do not identify with a label which attaches me to one child only.

On the same issue, Participant 3 said;

... I am involved .. lives of all my five children but government .. link me .. with one.. and label me with his support.

This finding agrees with research by Scourfield (2005) who concluded that policy has placed carers in a heroic discourse woven around concepts of love and obligate duty. The two male participants were forced by the death of the primary carer to take on the role and both were retired when they took the role. The researcher could not find any current evidence-based research into sibling caring for LD in retirement nor in adulthood (participants 5 and 10).   Kenny & McGilloway (2007) found that little is known about caring for siblings with LD. There are emotional and physical demands on the carer in looking after a co-resident person with LD (Forde et al 2004) and little is known on how this impacts the elderly carer. The researcher could not find current evidence-based research on LD and aging as is the case for the sibling, participant 5, looking after his older sister who is now forgetful and has reduced mobility. This agrees with the systematic review by Innes et al (2012) which revealed lack of robust research evidence on lives of older people with LD. Participants 5 and 10, the sibling carers, lead busy lives, which agrees with research results from Dew et al (2004) that the sibling carer deals with their own life changes and accommodate the caring role. Twigg and Atkin (1994) observed that caring occurs in kinship obligation underplayed by love between the carer and cared-for and a sense of responsibility by the carer. This research had similar findings from participants 5 and 10, the sibling carers when asked about institutionalizing, participant 5 said;

I will never put her into care as long as I can look after her. ... My mum and dad would turn in their graves!

Participant 10 on the same issue;

I did not want her to go into care... I grew up with her and I know her best second to my parents.....

This finding shows that the sibling participants are close to the cared-for which is unlike the results from Orsmond & Seltzer (2007) who suggested that siblings of those on the autistic spectrum are likely to be less close in relationship.

4.2.9   Challenging behaviour

Observational data suggested that participants have firm beliefs. They spoke with passionate conviction on things like frustration with LD communication problems when the carers cannot decipher communication and this causes of challenging behaviour. This finding concurs with the conclusion by Cogher (2005) that communication is one of the vulnerable areas of life. This implies that despite Watzlawich et al (1967) stating that all interactional behaviour in communication has a message value; there are times when carers are unable to understand how to give people with LD choice and control so that they are 'heard and understood', (Concannon, 2005), despite using the supported decision-making model (DH 2001). This, despite the fact that carers usually can communicate with people with LD with the 'third ear', (Feltman and Dryden 2004) to know the triggers, (Braithwaite 2001) for challenging behaviour. Issues of challenging behavior impact the carer's health and affect their wellbeing. Participant 1 shows issues which arise from this and how challenging they are for the carer;

times when I do not understand .. signs not adequate . Then I do not know what to do and even if I want to call someone, I don't know what to say is wrong. ..cannot get an appointment quickly.

Challenging behavior impacts community access as shown by participants 5, 8 and summed up by behaviour of participant 6's cared-for;

.. Kicking, punching, vomiting, spitting and smearing feaces ... the behavior that gets in the way of trying..other services ...

Participants 6 and 8 have young children with challenging behavior and hyper activity and their social workers are actively involved in their lives. A pilot study by George &Kidd (2011) assessed the validity of a modified Incredible Years Parent Training program as intervention for parents of children with moderate to severe LD. The results showed an increase in observed positive interactions. They concluded that the program may be a useful early intervention for children with a learning disability. This study did not ascertain which program participants 6 and 8's children were using although they were on a behavior training program.

The people participants 2 and 4 care for show elements of mental health problems which seem to agree with the findings of Kiernan et al (1995) who reported that three of four parents who received advice did not find it useful. Participant 2 has sought help from psychiatrists and has had training in management of the issues as her son has limited communication skills;

... He is always piling things ... mood swings... ……. says, 'Dad died, what am I going to do when you die as well?

The issues of mental health and challenging behavior can affect the emotional state of the carer (Sloper et al 2006). It also does not help if the carers cannot get a break because schools/respite centres and other service providers, who have trained experts, keep calling the carer during respite. These calls have important implications on the adequacy of information in the care plan being used by service providers. In formal care settings, a different paid carer takes care of one service user over a set period and takes a break but this is not the case with carers at home dealing with challenging issues. It is imperative that the preventive measures of the Care Act 2014 address the impact of challenging behaviour of people with LD on the carer to reduce care break down. Participant 3 talked about employment for those with LD;

...the community has expectations which some people with LD might not fulfill.... public banter can result in challenging behavior............

Participants, 3, 4, 2 and 5, showed themselves to be carers who are a resource (Twigg and Atkins 1994) and they highlight the need for public perception training and use of language which does not offend.

Participant 3 also raised issues of spending cuts and their effect on carers;

..... So services... are being cut and what replaces them does not meet my need... which sometimes is the only respite the carer has...

This finding agrees with the Learning Disability Coalition (2008) quantitative study with thematic analysis of 685 carers questionnaire on the effects of cuts in services on people with LD. The results showed the introduction or increase, in charges for services means that some people will not be able to afford them and will do without; people with LD had many good experiences of employment and inclusion in the community but there were problems for those who are 'too able' for services; and that there was frustration caused by insufficient employment support.

Coping Strategies

4.3.0   Care Sharing

Participant 1, 6, 7, 8 are lone carers whose relationships broke down, although 1, 7 and 8 still care share with the ex-partner. This finding agrees with research findings by Beresford (1995) that there are often relationship breakdowns among carers of people with LD. Six participants care share within the family, allowing the primary carer to take short breaks. This finding provides insight into the opportunities linked to development of intervention which builds on the strengths of all family members, as recommended by the DoH (2008) White Paper on LD. Participant 3 shows that family care sharing offers quality care with activities that interest the family member and the cared-for as well;

my family,.... working together around his needs... use each family member's strengths to work with him.....My son's siblings' children help him ....

Selwyn (2012) research in England described the findings of an analysis of the 2001 UK Population Census kinship care. This research has identified 2 sibling carers; male and female. The male sibling participant is retired and looking after his older sibling of the opposite sex. The female participant is looking after her younger, adult sibling of the same sex. O'Brien (2012) found evidence that relatives receive both less support and supervision from agencies than do foster parents. This research does not agree as both sibling participants in this research received full support from professionals although it did not make findings on supervision. The research by Selwyn (2012) and O'Brien (2012) were based on children and not specifically on LD and but they are the only research relevant to kinship care the researcher could find in the UK. Strozier (2012) study used the Dunst Family Support Scale (Dunst et al, 1994) to measure how social support changed for kinship caregivers who participated in support groups versus kinship caregivers who did not attend the support groups. Findings indicated that caregivers who attended support groups had greater increased social capital than those caregivers who did not as they were more likely to increase formal social supports such as parent groups, social groups/clubs, church members, professional helpers and agencies compared to an increase in informal support relatives, friends and children. This finding is echoed from the networks that participants 5 and 10 have although participant 5 has informal support as well.

4.3.1 Religion

The value of religion for the carer and the cared-for is summed up by participant 1;

I go to mass every Sunday morning ... He .. enjoys the church service in his own way. My faith carries me through difficult times....

Participant 10 shows the support from the religious groups;

Our pastor and a few church members visit often and she enjoys atmospheres of singing.

Participant 2;

...my assessment, we did not talk about religion. I go to church and sometimes ... comes... some of my church members (support) him. ...

These findings show that 8 out of 10 participants use religion/spirituality as a positive coping strategy (Chambers 2001). The fact that this coping strategy was not discussed during the CA for all 8 participants would appear to indicate contradiction between policy and practice as Social work deals with individuals from a strengths perspective (Saleeby 2009) but practitioners overlooked the strength from religion and therefore ignoring an important contributor to the carer well-being principle which the Care Act 2014 implemented. Practitioners should be committed to the whole person in environment approach taking a bio-psycho-social- spiritual view identifying resources important for coping, resilience and optimal development, (Canda and Furman 2010). In practice, social workers did not collect information about coping for the participants nor about the cared-for enjoying religious gatherings. They had a CA form which, from these findings, was not designed in partnership with carers. Bayat (2007) stated that professionals often fail to consider factors related to resilience. Koenig (2007) observed that religious practice influence health, mental health and social relationships and so spirituality should be responded to in a professional manner although some researchers object (Moss 2005, Wesiman 1997). This research's participants, mostly had their CA between 2005 and 2007. Although an increase in religiosity and spiritual support was associated with lower incidence of depression, increased self esteem and self-care (Murray- Swank et al 2006), the CA form for 2012 still did not collect such data. Research has noted that although the momentum for spiritually sensitive social work has grown rapidly recently, many practitioners remain unaware or suspicious (Canda and Furman 2010). Considering the huge amount of money carers save government, they will be effectively supported when practitioners and policy makers have knowledge and understanding of the factors that foster and promote coping strategies (Kuupelomaki et al (2004).

Formal Services

4.3.2 Respite

Participant 7 has not had respite because the cared-for changes her mind about accessing it. Participants 3, 10 and 8, have used the local Authority respite. The other participants, including participant 3 who later stopped accessing Local authority respite, would rather have family based respite. This finding agrees with Prosser & Moss (1996) who state that family, friends and neighbours are important in the lives of people with LD as they look after the disabled in the way the carer does, (Llewellyn et al 2003). This research concurs with the findings from Barr (2008) which showed significantly less stress in using home based short breaks where siblings spend time with the disabled sibling. The finding also agrees with that by Mencap (2006) that 8 out of 10 carers had never had respite. Participant 3 sums up the views about why carers want family based respite as the formal respite increases their stress (Hartley & Wells, 2003);

respite centre calls you many times .. A care plan fails to capture .. unforeseen details... The only real respite we have ..with siblings

This finding on respite triangulates with those from care sharing, work and education on issues of service providers calling the carer regularly. This brings to question the adequacy of the care plan and whether practitioners should revisit that document to take a fully inclusive cyclical lifespan approach. Research by Caldwell and Heller (2003), explored respite management and family support by relatives and level of control by 97 carers using respite and personal assistants. The study found that more control by family on respite management was associated with increased service satisfaction; increased community access of the service user; increased employment of mothers and that families employed friends, neighbours and other family members as this increased community access for the service user. This finding also agrees with Brown (2010) whose research on carers of people with LD recommended that respite services should be tailor made to individual families and called for innovation of events for carers and cared-for entertainment.

In this research, 7 participants had not used formal respite, although respite is meant to restore the carer's ability to care (Van Excel et al, 2006). This has serious implications on the nature of preventive measures which the Care Act 2014 implements, as respite is a preventive measure but carers are no happy with the service. The findings concur with the research by Mansell and Wilson (2009) which showed that carers were not satisfied with respite care services. Carers expressed fears based on the quality of respite care, its safety, how enjoyable it is for the person with LD and whether it was adequate in terms of providing the carer with a break (Shaw et al 2009). McConkey et al (2011) analysed national data on the use of respite breaks in the Republic of Ireland to examine the proportion of carers who had any access to breaks. The results showed that those people with severe disabilities were given priority; contact with social workers and community nurses increased the likelihood of receiving respite breaks; disabled adults aged 20–39 years were more likely than children to receive a respite break. In this research the three participants, 8, 10 and 3, who used local authority respite, had cared-for aged 11, 29 and 24 and two of them (participants 10 and 8) had constant contact with their social workers which agrees with the McConkey findings.

4.3.3   Worry with community Access

Participants 1, 2, 8 and 3 talked about inactivity and dietary issues which agree with the research by Melville (2007) that people with LD have obesity issues and lead inactive lives (Frey 2004). Participant 2 highlighted the flip side of diet in independent living proving the findings from Young et al (2007) that people with LD become exposed to health risks with the move to community living;

… was thin as a rack after eight months of living by himself. He can't cook, so he was ordering take out…. he got into debt …

This participant was dealing with the illness and then death of her spouse. She experienced 'Pile-up,' a complex set of changing conditions that add strain to her ability to cope with crisis events (Lavee et al, 1985). A cyclical lifespan care plan, which allows input from the carer, family service providers and professionals, should support carers to maintain well-being and achieve their outcomes through different life events. 'Pile-up' is a challenge for the Care Act 2014 preventive measures' ability to reduce care break down.

Participant 3 highlighted the problems of employment for people with LD and the extension of carers' worry into community living showing that caring includes a strong element of invisible caring and preparing for anticipated problems (Ekwall et al 2004). Yoong & Koritas (2012) carried out qualitative research with 12 carers of people with LD and concluded that caring was associated with financial insecurity and frustrations at the service system. The findings on worrying from participants 3, 2, 9 and 6 agree with the findings from Weeks et al (2008). Their mixed methods research with 43 parents showed that parents help children with LD to become productive and active members of society and they are interested in what their children can do. Participant 3 captures the worry, obesity issues and insecurity;

He now lives in a Housing Association…, I worry….. am always 'on call'. The burden of care .. …takes on a different dimension of supervision.

Participant 3;

I am aware.. that the shifting community environment presents challenges for people with LD …. but the community has expectations which some people with learning disabilities might not fulfill. My son, big as he is,… When he cannot, they ask rhetorical questions like, 'Are you stupid or what ?' My son does not understand why he is being insulted because most of his life has been in environments which have shown him patience, nurturing and encouragement….public banter can result in challenging behavior and the public then question access to the community. I always find myself confronting such comments…..There is need to sensitise employers and the public.'.

These findings is complimentary to the nurturing service provider environments for people with learning disabilities. They also show that transition of people with LD creates new frontiers of care worry and agree with research by Graungaard & Skov (2006) who proved that parents want services which offer the respect and reliability that family support provides. The findings also show the tension between inclusion and intellectual capital of people with learning disabilities, (Clifford 2012). Intellectual life is deeply individual and collective at the same time, diverse and needs societal support to flourish as atrophy of any life is unhealthy, (Agre 2001). People with LD have an intellectual life which is harnessed in society, as was recently shown by their excellent participation for the first time at the 2012 Olympics. The supreme test of all political and industrial arrangements shall be the contribution they make to all-round growth of every member of society, (Dewey 1920). The community access of people with LD should lead to their personal growth in meaningful employment. This finding agrees with the Learning Disability Coalition quantitative study with 685 carers on the effects of cuts in services on people with LD in 2008. The results showed that people with LD had many good experiences of employment and inclusion in the community. The frustration caused by insufficient employment support; the tension between societal expectations based on someone's physicality and public banter which can result in challenging behavior seem to point to the need for more public /employer awareness training.

This research has found that people with learning disabilities also assert themselves and refuse to partake in community access or limit their own access. It is a challenge for service providers and practitioners to establish how much of this refusal is linked to the personality, stigma and public bunter. Is there mismatch between the respectful, nurturing and caring environment of the family and that of the community in general as perceived by the intellectual capital of people with learning disabilities? No matter their level of intellectual capital as measured by the IQ, people with learning disabilities can perceive stigma and body language which is negative towards them as this is part of 'personhood' Kitwood (1997). Participant 7 's views are shared by participants 10, 9;

I tried to engage her in activities in the community but she was unwilling to do them and she does not like crowds……

Community access is limited by lack of understanding by those with LD as to why the community is invading the home environment from personal assistants as shown by participant 5;

…. the befriending service… It did not work .. because … did not understand why the stranger was there…I employed another church member.

Research has shown that carers tend to employ family, friends or church members because people with LD prefer to work with those they are familiar with.

4.4.0 Purpose of the study.

This researcher set out to find the answers to two research objectives which form the basis of this study;

- Exploring the experiences of Carers for people with learning difficulties who have had their needs assessed and have received service.

- Exploring whether the support/ services received by the carers are meeting their needs.

The research has explored the experiences of carers of people with LD who had their needs assessed. Its findings, in terms of difficulties of assembling a sample, proved the findings of Mencap (2006) that 1 in 3 had not had a CA. The findings also agree with Wing (1981) on the prevalence of males in LD; and of the NHS Executive (1999) that people with LD have additional impairments as shown in Table 1; that death of a family member affects the disabled as proved by Dew et al (2004). This research found that older parents care for adult children as proved by Weekes et al (2008). The new finding was in older sibling looking after older adult sibling and adult sibling caring for an adult sibling. The study proved the carer's third shift, care worrying, (Hochschild, 1997; Cheung, 2004) linked to community access. The study also proved what Cuskelly (2006) found that people with LD live longer. Participants' many roles did not allow free time to take up all services, education, work and respite being offered by the Carers Assessment and in most cases those are not services that meet their needs. This finding has important implications on the type of preventive services available to achieve carers' well-being from the Care Act 2014. All the participants in the research took part in leisure activities as offered through the CC. Carers felt the assessment process itself was a great chance to talk about themselves and they felt that focus was on their needs although there was a form being filled in. The generic support services are not meeting carers' needs. Carers are interested in short courses such as pottery, massage and health related courses or management of challenging behavior, etc which are relevant to their lives, help them to cope or to learn a new skill but not in formal long courses. Carers and people with learning disabilities use religion for community access, respite, care sharing and coping. Carers want family/ friends based respite as it reduces their worry. There are challenges of the intellectual capital of people with LD in employment. Worrying is associated with formal respite, supported living and work. Short breaks are used to catch up on sleep or chores. There is kinship caring in LD. Carers struggle with the mental health issues of those with LD. Cross-generational caring for people with LD and sensitizing of the issues by grandparents is an important new finding. The Care Act 2014 takes a whole family approach in Carer's Assessment which should pick up cross-generational carers in the care sharing chain in working with the family strength. It should incorporate all the support services that the family work with to enable practitioners to make care plans with family and support network that reduce the need for service providers calling on carers and reducing carers' well-being and participation in work, education, training, social and economic activities.

Chapter 5   CONCLUSION AND RECOMMENDATIONS

5.1 Introduction
This study identified 5 major themes. This chapter outlines the research limitations and makes suggestions for ideas of further research which has stemmed from the results. It makes conclusions to the study with recommendations.

5.2 Consideration of research limitation
The study included a small sample of 10 carers of people with LD living in a borough in North London. The study used a convenience sample which is unlikely to be representative of the larger population caring for people with learning disabilities. Sampling was biased as participants were recruited from those who attended carers meetings. Those who, for whatever reason do not attend the meetings, were not invited to participate in the research. The small sample and this bias, limit the generalizability of the findings. The results represent the views of those carers of people with LD who attend services offered by the CC and who had a Carers Assessment. Although efforts were made to recruit from different socio economic and cultural backgrounds, it is possible that some groups were over/underrepresented. The sample consisted of carers

that met these criteria, carers of people with LD who had a CA, were willing to be recorded and volunteering to participate in the study. There could be major differences of view points from those who fit two criteria but were unwilling to be recorded and did not volunteer; and different view points from those who fit all criteria but were unable to attend Carers' Centre meetings. Even with its short comings and lack of genalisability, the findings of this research add to the body of knowledge and have important implications on choice and control in partnership work to achieve the well-being principle and nature of preventive measures of the Care Act 2014.

5.3 Ideas for further research

Although this research provided insight into issues; kinship caring in LD, mental health of LD, cross-generational caring for LD, employment of people with LD, religiosity as a coping strategy for carers and as relaxation for the cared-for, rethinking care plans, seeing carers as educators, respite with family /friends, the intellectual capital of people with LD and its commodification, older carers of people with LD; these results cannot be generalized because of the small sample. Further research to explore the extent of these issues among carers is needed. It should be easier to find a sample as the 2014 Care Act makes it a duty for the Local Authority to assess and meet the needs of the service user and carer. Further research is needed to explore the follow up participants were expecting after their CA.

5.4 Conclusion and recommendations

Despite its limitations, the current study has important implications for research, for assessing carers and their expectations and for care planning in LD. The implications extend to co-production and on-going support for carers of people with LD. Ramsden (2010) says co-production for carers means transferring more power and control to carers to decide respite, education, work and leisure by developing innovative ways of working in carer-led partnership with social services so that meaningful change takes place at the caring level; and valuing carers as assets with intelligences that have been gained which can be harvested to educate others from synergetic partnerships.

The study identified LD issues in the community and issues with the name carer and respite dissatisfaction. In the light of the 'well-being principle' from the Care Act 2014, it is recommended that the study is repeated in many different locations with larger samples using additional methods of data collection for triangulation because the following themes that emerged need to be tested in larger samples;

Telling their story
Professionals working with carers in CA need to develop the assessment tool with the carers and to give feedback so that assessment is an on-going process to pick up changing lifespan needs for the carer and cared-for; this approach would show respect for the 'personhood' of the carer and cared-for. The research suggests that participants overall had positive impact from social networking after referral to the CC. Practitioners and service providers need to think in terms of true partnership in order to give carers services that are meaningful to them.

Personal development
The results strengthen the knowledge base of carers of people with LD showing that they are interested in self-development. They purposefully choose what can fit into their schedule of caring and other responsibilities. Practitioners and policy makers need to be aware that education in society can benefit from the knowledge and skills gained by carers in terms of dealing not just with issues of LD but with raising siblings and grandchildren.

Life on hold
Participants put their life on hold to care, risking their health and dealing with challenging behavior and their multi roles. This is an area where a lot of support is needed and a partnership approach would produce the best outcomes especially with the preventive support services which the Care Act 2014 is putting in place for carers to have positive outcomes in well-being.

Coping strategies
Professionals need to understand, and acknowledge the carers' coping strategies and incorporate them in action plans. Spending cuts closed Carers Centres and some centres for the people with LD which aided carers daily coping with short breaks. This has affected the care sharing chain. Preventive support services being implemented by the Care Act 2014 should incorporate the coping strategies that carers rely on to prevent care breakdown and early placement in residential care for the carer, the cared-for and people in the care chain. A whole family approach to Carers Assessment should identify the carer's support network.

Formal services
Social services should invest more effort into partnership work to redefine the word carer and work with policy makers, carers and employers to assist in the employment for people with LD. Practitioners need to reformulate care plans to include life span changes and ways that families deal with challenging behavior to improve formal service provision and reduce the need for service providers to call carers during carers' respite. This means

involving carers and giving them control over their respite. Comprehensive family-led respite services which meet the carers' need for a break and are more meaningful to the cared-for would meet carers' needs. Effective partnership should be able to find ways to ensure that the intellectual capital of people with LD is harnessed commercially in respectful atmospheres that allow for their economic and social growth. It is worth noting that all participants enjoyed the Carer's Assessment which is a positive pointer on the work of professionals.

REFERENCES AND BIBLIOGRAPHY

Abrahams, M. S., (2009) The well sibling: Challenges and possibilities. American Journal of Psychotherapy, 2009, 63 (4), pp 305- 331.

Agre, P. E., Supporting the intellectual life of a democratic society. Ethics and Information Technology,2001,3 (4) ABI/INFORM Research page 289.

Ahuja, A.S., & Williams, P., Involving patients and their carers in educating and training practitioners. Journal of Child and adolescent Psychiatry, July 2005, 18(4), pp 374- 380.

Al-Janabi, H., Terry, N., Coast, J., QALYS and carers. Pharmaco Economics, Dec 2011,12 , pp 1015-23.

Arksey, H. Glendinning, C. (2007) Combining work and care: Carers' decision-making in the context of competing policy pressures. Social Policy & Administration, 42(1), pp1-18

February 2008. [Online] Available on http://onlinelibraary.wiley.com/doi/101111/j.1467-9515.2007.00587.x/ full(Accessed 22 September 2011.

Arksey, H., & Hirst, M., Unpaid Carers Access to and use of primary care services. Health Care Research and development, April 2005, 6 (2), pp 101 – 116.

Aronson, J. (1992). A pragmatic view of Thematic Analysis. The Qualitative Report, 2 (1), Spring 1994. [Online] Available at http://www.nova.edu/ssss/QR/BackIssues/OR2-1/aronson.html accessed 26 October 2011 (Accessed 28 October 2011).

Ashworth (1996) Bracketing in phenomenology: Renouncing assumption in hearing about students cheating. International Journal of Qualitative Studies in Education. 1999, 12 (6), pp 707 – 721.

Atkinson, R., (1998) Exploring diverse interview types. Thousand Oaks, CA: Sage.

Barr, O., Gilgunn, J., Kane, T., Moore, G., Health screening for people with learning disabilities by a community learning disability nursing service in N. Ireland. Journal of Advanced nursing, June 1999, 29 (6), pp 1482- 1491

Barr , O., (2008) In Mansell, I., & Wilson, C., Current perceptions of respite care: experience of family and informal carers of people with a learning disability. Journal of intellectual disabilities, December 2009, 13 (4), pp255 – 267.

Bayat, M., Evidence of resilience in families of children with autism. Journal of Intellectual Disabilities Research, September 2007, 51 (9), pp 702- 714.

Beauchamp, T.L., Curry, L.A., Devers, K. J., (1982) Qualitative Data Analysis for health services research: developing Taxonomy, Themes and Theory. Baltimore: John Hopkins University Press.

Beck, A., Daley, D., Hastings, R.P., Stevenson, J., Mothers' expressed emotion towards children with or without intellectual disabilities. Journal of Intellectual Disability Research, August 2004, 48 (7), pp 628 -638.

Ben-Zur, H., (2005) in Ben-Zur, H., Coping styles and affect. International Journal of stress management, May 2009, 16 (2), pp 87 – 101.

Bernard, H. R., (1988) Research Methods in cultural Anthropology. London: Sage Publications.

Beresford, B., (1995) Expert opinions: A national survey of parents caring for a severely disabled child. York: The Polity Press.

Beresford, P., Shamash, M., Forrest, V., Turner, M., (2005) Developing social care: service user's vision for adult support. The Policy Press: London.

Blomquist, K.B., (2006) Health, Education, Work and independence of young adults with disabilities. Journal of orthopedic Nursing, 25 (3), pp 168- 187.

Blumer, M., (1976) In Waters- Adams, S., (2006) Action Research in education. Available onlinewww.edu.plymouth.ac.uk/resined/actionresearch (Accessed June 2012).

Blumer, M., (1969) in Coffey, A., Delamont, S., Lofland, J., & Lofland, L., (eds) (2007). Handbook of ethnography. London: Sage Publications.

Boyce, G. C., & Barnett, W. S., (1993) Siblings of persons with mental retardation: A historical perspective and recent findings. In; Stoneman, Z., & Berman, P. W., (eds) The effects of mental retardation, disability and illness on sibling relationships: research issues and challenges, pp 145-184) Baltimore: Paul, H. Brookes.

Boyatzis, R. E., (1998) Thematic Analysis and Code development. Thousand Oaks, CA: Sage Publications.

Bradley, E. H., Curry, L.A., Devers, K.J., Qualitative Data Analysis for Health Services Research: Developing Taxonomy, Themes and Theory. Health Services Research, August 2007, 42 (4), pp 1758 – 1772.

Bradshaw, J. (2001) Complexity of Staff Communication and Reported Level of understanding Skills in Adults with Intellectual Disabilities. Journal Of Intellectual Disability Research, 24 (3), pp 233-243.

Braithwaite, R., (2001) Managing Aggression. London: Routledge.

Brown, K., Carers Respite Needs – engagement exercise in Nottingham City. In NHS Nottingham City 13 October 2010.

Buckner, L. & Yeandle, S. (2005) Working below potential: women and part time work. Equal Opportunities Commission: Sheffield.

Buckner, L ., & Yeandle, S., (2007) Valuing and Supporting Carers. 4th report 2007-2008. London: House of Commons.

Buckner , L., & Yeandle, S., (2011) in Carers UK and Leeds University (2011) Valuing Carers. Leeds: Leeds University Press.

Burton, M., (2006) Grounding constructions of carers: exploring the experiences of carers through a grounded approach. British Journal of Social Work, 2008, 38, pp 493-506.

Burton- Smith, R., McVilly, K.R., Yazbeck, M., Parmenter, T.R., Tsutsui, T., (2006) Service and support needs of Australian carers supporting a family member with a disability at home. Journal of Intellectual and Developmental Disabilities, 2009, 34 (3), pp 239 – 247.

Buyck, J.F., Bonnaud, S., Boumendi, L.A., Andrieu, S., (2011) Informal care-giving and self reported mental and physical health: results from the Gazel Cohort study. American Journal of Public Health. Oct 2011, 101 (10), pp 1971 – 1979.

Brylewski, J., & Duggan, L., (2004) Antipsychotic medication for challenging behavior in people with leaning disability. The Cochrane Database of systematic Review 3. London: John Wiley & Sons.

Canda, E. R., (2008) In Canda, E. R., & Furman, L. D., (2009) Spiritual Diversity in social work Practice: the heart of help. Oxford: Oxford University Press.

Canda, E. R., and Furman, L.D., (2010) in Stirling, B., Furnman, L.D., Benson, P.W., Canda, E.R., and Grimwood, C., (2010) A comparative survey of Aetearoa New Zealan and U. K Social workers on the role of religion and spirituality in practice. BJSW, 2010, 40(2), pp 602-621.

Caldwell, J., & Heller, T., (2003) Management of respite and personal assistant services in a consumer directed family support program. Journal of Intellectual Disability Research, May 2003, 47 (4-5), pp 352-367.

Caples, M., & Sweeney, J., (2010). Quality of life: a survey of parents of children and adults with intellectual disabilities who are availing of respite care. British Journal of Learning Disabilities, March 2011, 39 (1), pp 64 – 72.

Carers (recognitions and services) Act 1995, available online at < www.lukeclements.co.uk/resources-index/files/PDF%2010.pdf> Accessed 29 July 2012.

Carers UK (2003) Missed Opportunities: the impact of new rights for carers. London: Carers UK.

Carers UK (2005) Carers and the digital divide. London: Carers UK.

Carers UK (2009) Clements, L., Carers and their rights: the law relating to carers. London: Carers UK.

Carers UK and Leeds University, (2011) Valuing Carers. Leeds: Leeds University Press.

Chambers, M.(2001) Exploring the emotional support needs and coping strategies of family carers. Journal of Psychiatric and mental health nursing, April 2001, 8(2), pp 99-106.

Charmaz , K.,(1995) Reducing fragmentation in Qualitative research. London: Blackwell Publications.

Carmichael, F., Hulme, C., Sheppard, S., and Connell, S., Work –life imbalance: informal care and paid employment in the UK. Feminist Economics, 14(2), April 2008, 3 – 35.

Catherall, C., & Iphofen, R., (2006) In Kearney, P. M., & Griffin, T., Between joy and sorrow: being a parent of a child with developmental disability issues and issues in nursing practice. Nursing and Management. 2007. Available online www.nursing2007 critical care.com (Accessed 21 September 2011)

Cheung, J. (2004). Caring as worrying: the experience of spousal carers. Journal of Advanced Nursing, September 2004, 47(5), pp 475-482.

Chung, B.G., Schneider, B., (2001) Serving multiple masters: role conflict experienced by service employees. Journal of Services Marketing, 2002, 16 (1), pp 70-87.

Cicirelli, V. G., (1995) Sibling Relationships across the lifespan. New York: Plenum Press.

Clifford, S., (2012) Making disability public in deliberate democracy. Contemporary Political Theory, May 2012, 11(2), pp 211-228.

Cogher, L., (2005) Communication with people with learning disabilities. In Grant, G., Goward, P., Richardson, M., and Rancharan, P., Learning disabilities: a life cycle approach to valuing people. Berkshire: Open University.

Concannon, L., (2005) in Blow, B., Empowering to disempower: a dilemma when working with adults with learning disabilities. Anthropology Matters, 2009.

Collins, E. C., & Green, J. L., (1990) Basics of Qualitative research. New York: Seabury.

Cuskelly, M., & Gunn, P., (1993) Mental reports of behavior of siblings of children with Down syndrome. American Journal of Mental Retardation, 35 (2), pp 114 – 123.

Cuskelly, M., (2006) in Rowbotham, M., Cuskelly, M., & Caroll, A., (2011) Sustainable care giving? Demands upon and resources of female carers of adults with Intellectual Disabilities. Journal of women and Aging, 2011, 23 (2), pp 129 – 148.

Deb, S., Hare, M., Prior, L., Symptoms of dementia among adults with Down's syndrome: a qualitative study. Journal of Intellectual Disabilities Research, Sept 2009, 51 (9), pp 726 – 739.

Deimling, G. T., (1992) Respite use and care giver well being in families caring for stable and declining AD patients. Journal of Gerontological Social Work, 18 (1/2), pp117 -134.

Deimling, G. T., (1992) Bendini Family care givers and leisure: an oxymoron? Research Update. Parks and Recreation, 37 (1), pp 25 – 31.

Department of Health. (2001) Valuing People. A new strategy for learning disability for 21 century. London: HMSO.

Department of Health (2008) Carers at the heart of 21st century families and communities. Available on < www.dh.gov.uk/publications> Accessed 12 August 2012.

Department of Health and Department Of Works and Pensions Survey of Carers in Households, 2009-2010.[Online] Available at< http://www.esds.ac.uk/doc/6768/mrdoc/UKDA_Study_6768_Information.htm> (Accessed 23 September 2011).

Denzin, N., (1989) in Denzin, N., & Lincoln, Y., (eds) (1994) Entering the field of Qualitative research. Thousand Oaks: Sage Publications.

Dew, A., Llewellyn, G., Balandin, S., Post-parental care: a new generation of sibling-carers. Journal of Intellectual & Developmental Disability, June 2004, 29 (2), pp 176 – 179.

Dewey J (1920) Reconstruction in philosophy. New York: Holt

DeVault, M. L., (1990) Talking and listening from women's standpoint: Feminist Strategies for interviewing and analysis. Social Problems, 1990, 37, pp 96 – 116.

Doo, S., & Wing, Y.K., (2006) Sleep problems of children with pervasive developmental disorders: correlation with parental stress. Developmental Medicine & Child Neurology, Aug 2006, 48 (8), pp 650 – 655.

Dunst, C. J., Trivette, C. M., & Hamby, D. W., (1994) Measuring social support in families with young children with disabilities. Supporting and strengthening families, 1994, 1, pp152 – 160.

Dyson, L., (2010) Unanticipated effects of children with learning disabilities. Learning Disability Quarterly, 2010, 33 (1), pp 43 – 55.

Ekwall, A., Sivberg, b., & Hallberg, I., (2004) Dimensions of informal care and quality of life among elderly family caregivers. Scandinavian Journal of Caring Sciences, 18, pp 239 -248.

Ellison, C. E., & Levin, J. S., (1998) The religion Health connection: evidence Theory, and Future directions. Journal of Health and Religion. Available online< http://csrs.nd.edu/assets/59929/ellison_and_levin> Accessed 6 September 2012

Emerson, E., et al (1998) in Bromley, J., Hare, D. J., Davidson, K., Emerson, E., (1998) Mothers supporting children with autistic spectrum disorders: social support, mental health status and satisfaction with services. Autism, Dec 2004, 8 (4), pp 409 – 423.

Emerson, E., (2005) Underweight, obesity and exercise among adults with intellectual disabilities in supported accommodation in Northern England. Journal of Intellectual Disability Research, 2005, 49 (2), pp 134 – 143.

Engel, R. J., & Schutt, R.K., (2009) Social Work Research. London: Sage Publications.

Epel, E. S., Blackburn, E. H., Lin, J., Dhadgar, F. S., Adler, N. E., Morrow, J. D., & Cawthon, R. M., (2004) Accelerated telomere shortening response to life stress. Proceedings of the National Academy of Sciences of the United States of America, 101, Pp 17312- 17315.

Family Group Conferencing. Available online at < http://www.frg.org.uk/involving - families>

Felltham, C., and Dryden, W., (2004) Dictionary of Counselling. 2nd ed. London: Whurr.

Forde, H., Lane, H., McCloskey, D., McManus, V., Tierney, E., (2004) Link Family Support: an evaluation of an in-home support service. Journal of Psychiatry Mental Health Nursing; 2004, 11, pp 698 – 704.

Frey, B., (2004) In Melville, C.A., Cooper, S.A., Morrison, J., Allan, L., Smiley, E., & Williamson, A., The prevalence of obesity in adults with intellectual disabilities. Journal of Applied Research in Intellectual Disability, 21 (5), pp 425 – 437.

Fuller, R., & Petch, A., (1995) Practitioner Research: the reflexive social worker. Basingstoke: Open University Press.

Gabanillas In Roodin, P., Intergenerational Relationships: one of many perspectives of the intergenerational relationships. Journal of Intergenerational Relationships, 2011, 9 (2), pp 121-127.

Garfinkel, H. (1967) Studies in Ethno methodology. Englewood Cliffs: NJ: Prentice Hall.

George, L. K., Ellison, C. G., Larson, D. B., (2002) Explaining the relationship between religious involvement and health. Psychological Inquiry, 2002, 13 (3), pp 190 – 200.

George, C., Kidd, G., Effectiveness of a parent training program adapted for children with learning disability. Learning Disability Practice, Oct 2011, 14 (8), pp 18 – 24.

Gergen , K. J., (1995) Language as a vehicle of power: social construct and the transformation of identity politics. New York City: New School for Social Research.

Glassner, B., & Loughlin, T., (1987) In West, W., & Talib, M. A., Hearing what research participants are really saying: the influence of researcher cultural identity. Journal of Counselling & Psychotherapy Research. Jan 2008, 2 (4), pp 253-258.

Gillham, B., (2005) Research Interviewing: the range of techniques. Open University Press: Maidenhead.

Gitlin, L. N., Hodgson, N., Jutkowitz, E., Pizzi, L., (2003) The cost effectiveness of nonpharmacologic intervention for individuals with dementia and family caregivers: the tailored activity program. American Journal of Geriatric Psychiatry, June 2010, 18 (6), pp 510 – 519.

Glendinning, C., Arksey, H., Jones, K., Moran, N., Netten, A., Rabiee, P., (2009) The individual budget projects: impact and outcomes for carers. York: Social Policy Research.

Glendinning, C. (12September 2011). Caring for people at home: developments in paid and unpaid care. Best Practice workshop. Brussels. SPRU. University of York: York.

Grasta, A., Spiller, M. J., Holt, G., Joyce, T., Hardy, S., and Bouras, N.,

Developing a Mental Health Guide for Families and Carers of People with Intellectual

Disabilities. Journal of Applied Research in Intellectual Disabilities, 2007, 20, pp77–86.

Graungaard & Skov (2006) Why do we need a diagnosis? A qualitative study of parents experience coping and needs when the newborn child is severely disabled. Available online at < http://www.aafesp.org.br/biblioteca> Accessed 3 July 2012.

Grbich, C. (2007) Qualitative Data Analysis: An Introduction. Sage: London.

Hames, A., & Rollings, C., (2009) A group for the parents and carers of children with severe intellectual disabilities and challenging behavior. Educational & Child Psychology, 2009, 26 (4), pp 47 – 54.

Hartley, L., & Wells, J.S.G., (2003) The meaning of respite care to mothers of children with learning disabilities: two Irish case studies. Journal of Psychiatry Mental Health Nursing, 10, pp 335 – 342.

Hassall, R., Rose, J., & McDonald, J. M., (2005) Parental Stress in mother of children with intellectual disabilities: the effects of parental cognitions in relation to child characteristics and family support. Journal of Intellectual Disability Research, June 2005, 49 (6), pp 405 – 418.

Hatton, C., (2002) Psychosocial interventions for adults with intellectual disabilities and mental health problems: A Review. Journal of Mental Health, 11 (4), pp 357 – 374.

Hayman, F., (2005) Helping carers care: an education program for rural carers of people with a mental illness. Australas Psychiatry, June 2005, 13 (2), pp 148 – 158.

HCPC code of practice <www.gscc.org.uk>

Heller, T., & Factor, A., (1993) Aging family caregivers; Support, resources and changes in burden and placement desire. American Journal of Mental Retardation. 98, pp 417 – 426.

Heller, T., Miller, A. B., & Factor, A., (1997) Adults with mental retardation as supports to their parents; effects on parental care giving appraisal. Mental Retardation, 35, pp 338 – 346.

Herbert, R., (2007) Religion and Depression. In Blazer, D. G., religious beliefs in practice and mental health outcomes: What is the research question? American Journal of Geriatric Psychiatry, April 2007, 15 (4), pp 269 - 272.

Heron, C., (1998) Working with carers. London: Jessica Kingsley Publishers.

Hirst, M., (2004) Health inequalities and informal care: prospective population based study. Social Policy Unit: University of York.

Hochschilds, A. R., (1997) In Southerton, D., Squeezing Time: allocating practices, coordinating networks and scheduling society. Time Society, March 2003, 12 (1), pp 1-25.

Holstein, J.A. and Gubrium, J.F. (2003) Qualitative Research Practice. London: Sage.

Hubert, J., Family carers views of services for people with learning disabilities from Black and minority ethnic groups: a qualitative study of 30 families in south London borough. Disability & Society. August 2006, 21 (3), pp 259-272.

Innes, A., McCabe, L., Watchman, K., Caring for older people with intellectual disability: a systematic review.; Aug 2012, 72 (4), pp 286 – 295.

Janesick, V. J., (1998) Choreography of qualitative research design, minuets, improvisations and crystallization. In Denzin, N. K., & Lincoln, Y.S., (2003) Strategies of qualitative inquiry. 2nd ed. London: Sage.

Janicki, M. P., Davidson, P.W., Henderson, C. M., McCallion, P., Taets, J. D., Force, T., Sulkes, S. B., Frangenberg, E., Ladrigan, P. M.,(2002) Health characteristics and health services utilization in older adults with intellectual disability living in community residences. Journal of Intellectual Disability Research, May 2004; 46 (4), pp 287 – 298.

Jewell, T. C., & Stein, C. H., (2002) Parental influence on sibling care giving for people with severe mental illness. Community Mental Health Journal, 2002, 38 (1), pp 17 – 33.

Joen, Y., Brodaty, H., Chesterton, J., (2005) Respite Care for Caregivers and people with mental illness: literature review. Journal of Advanced Nursing, Feb 2005, 49 (3), pp 297 – 306.

Jones, A. Jeyasingham, D. & Rajasooriya, S. 2002. Invisible Families: The strengths and needs of black families in which young people have caring responsibilities. Joseph Rowntree Foundation. London: The Polity Press

Johnson, R. W., & Lo Sasso, A. T. (2006). The impact of elder care on women's labour supply. Inquiry, 43(3), 195–210.

Jorgensen, D. Parsons, M. Jacobs, S. (2009) The experience of informal caregivers in New Zealand. University of Auckland: New Zealand.

Keeley, B., & Clarke, M., (2002) Carers Speak out project report on findings and recommendations. London: Princess Royal Trust for Carers.

Kenny, K., & McGilloway, S., (2007) Caring for children with learning disabilities: an exploratory study of parental strain and coping. British Journal of Learning Disability, 35, pp 221-228.

Kiernan, C., Reeves, D., & Alborz, A., (1995) The use of anti-psychotic drugs with adults with learning disabilities and challenging behavior. Journal of Intellectual Disability Research, Aug 1995, 39 (4), pp 263 – 274.

Kinship Care Alliance, Sept 2011. Available online at http://www.frg.org.uk/involving-families (Accessed 28 September 2012)

Koenig, H. G., (2007) Religion and depression in older medical inpatients. American Journal of Geriatric Psychiatry, April 2007,15 (4), pp 282 – 291.

Kuupplelomaki, M., Sasaki, A., Yamada, K., Asakawa, N., Shimanouchi, S., (2004) Coping strategies of family carers of older relatives in Finland. Journal of Clinical Nursing, Sept 2004, 13 (6), pp 698-706.

Lazaro, N., Molto, M. L., & Sanchez, R., (2004) Paid Employment and unpaid caring in Spain. Applied Economics, 2004, 36 (9), pp 977 – 986.

Lavee Y., McCubbin, H. I., & Patterson, J. M., (1985) The double ABCX model of family stress and adaptation: an empirical test by analysis of structural equations with latent variations. Journal of Marriage and Family, 1985, 47 (4), pp 811 – 823.

Lecavalier, L., Leone, S., & Wiltz, J., (2006) The impact of behavior problems on caregivers stress in young people with autism spectrum disorder. Journal of Intellectual Disability Research, March 2006, 50 (3), pp 172 – 183.

Lennox, N. G., & Kerr, M. P., (1997) Primary Health care and people with intellectual Disability: the evidence base. Journal of Intellectual Disability Research, 1997, 41, pp 365 – 372.

Learning Disability Coalition (2008) Tell it like it is. Available online at www.learningdisabilitycoalition.org.uk (Accessed 13 July 2012)

Leggett, A.N., Zarit, S., Taylor, A., & Galvin, J.E., (2010). Stress and burden among caregivers of patients with lewy body dementia. The Gerontologist, 2011, 51(1), pp 76-85.

Leininen, A.,(2011) Masters of their own time? Working carers visions about combining retirement and caring. In Nygard, C., Savinainem, M.m Kirsi, T., & Lumme-Sandt, K., (eds) Age Management during the life course; proceedings of the 4th symposium on work ability, 2011, pp 246-254. Tampere, Finland. Tampere University Press.

Llewellyn, G., Gething, L., Kendig, H., & Cant, R., (2003) Invisible carers facing an uncertain future. Sydney: University of Sydney.

Llewellyn, G., McCannell, D., Gething, L., Cant, R., Kendig, H., (2010) Health status and coping strategies among older parent carers of adults with learning disabilities in Australia. Research, development and disability, 2010, 31 (6), pp 1176 – 1186.

Lister, P. G., (2003) It's like you cant be a whole person, a mother who studies! Lifelong learning: mature women students with caring commitments in social work education. Social Work Education: The International Journal, 2003, 22 (2), pp 125 – 138.

LoBiondo-Wood, G., & Haber, J., (1998) Nursing research methods, critical appraisal and utilization. University of Michigan: Mosby.

MacDonald, H., & Callery, P., (2004) Short breaks: Different meanings of respite: a study of parent carers, nurses and social workers caring for children with complex needs. Child, Care, Health and Development, May 2004, 30 (3), pp 279 – 288.

Manchester City Council Adult Social Care (2009) Carers Assessment Survey. Available at< http//www.thilocalactpersonal.org.uk/ - library. (Accessed 15 September 2012)

Mansell, I., & Wilson, C., Current perceptions of respite care: experiences of family and informal carers of people with a learning disabilities. Journal of intellectual Disabilities, December 2009, 13(4), pp 255-267.

Mark, P., (1996) Towards rich and valid qualitative design and analysis. Available online at < www.unisa.ac.za/contents> (Accessed 17 August 2012)

Matthews, B., and Ross, L., (2010) Research Methods: a practical guide for social sciences. Pearson Education Limited: London.

McGill, P., Papachristoforou, E., and Cooper, V., (2005) Support for family carers of children and young people with developmental disabilities and challenging behavior. Child: Care, Health &Development, 2006, 32 (2) pp159-165

McConkey, R., Kelly, F., Craig, S., Access to respite break for families who have a relative with intellectual disabilities: a national survey. Journal of Advanced Nursing, Jun 2011, 67 (6), pp 1349 – 1357.

McNally, S., Ben-Shlomo, Y., & Newman, S., (1999) The effects of respite care on informal carers well-being: a systematic review. Disability & Rehabilitation, Jan 1999, 21 (1), pp 1 - 14.

Melville, C.A., Hamilton, S., Miller, S., Boyle, B., Robinson, N., Pert, C., and Hankey, C.R., (2008) Carer knowledge and perceptions of Healthy Lifestyles for adults with intellectual disabilities. 304 Journal of Applied Research in intellectual Disabilities, 2008, 22., pp 298-306.

Melville, C. A., Cooper, S. A., Morrison, J., Allan, L., Smiley, E., Williamson, A., (2007) The prevalence of obesity in adults with learning disabilities. Journal of applied research in Intellectual Disability, Sept 2008, 21 (5), pp 425 – 437.

Mencap (2006) Breaking Point: families in need of a break. Available online at www.learningdisabilitycoalition.org.uk (Accessed 27 August 2012).

Middleton, L., (1997) Services for disabled children: interpreting the perspective of social workers. Children and Families Social Work Journal, Nov 1998, 3 (4), pp 239 – 246.

Miles, M., & Huberman, A., (1994) Qualitative data analysis. (2nd ed). Thousand Oaks, CA: Sage Publications.

Miller, G., In Miller, G., & Barbour, R. S., (2001) Checklist for improving rigour in qualitative research: a case of the tail wagging the dog. British Medical Journal, May 2001, 322 (7294), pp 1115 – 1117.

Minnes, P., Woodford, L. M., & Passey, J., (2007) in Rowbotham, M., Cuskelly, M., & Caroll, A., (2011) Sustainable care giving? Demands upon and resources of female carers of adults with Intellectual Disabilities. Journal of women and Aging, 2011, 23 (2), pp 129 – 148.

Minnes, P. M., & Woodford, L. M., (2004) Well-being in aging parents caring for an adult with a developmental disability. Journal on developmental Disabilities, 11, pp 47-66.

Moss, B., (2005) Religion and Spirituality. Lyme Regis, Dorset: Russell House.

Montgomery, RJV. Ronda, J.V., Kwak, J., Kosloski, K., O'Connell Valuchi, K., (2011) Effects of TCARE ® Intervention on caregiver burden and depressive symptoms: preliminary Findings from a randomised controlled study. Journals of Gerontology Series B- Psychological Sciences and Social Sciences, 66 (5), pp 640-647.

Morse, J. M., (2006) Biased Reflections: Principles of sampling and analysis in Qualitative enquiry (pp53-60). In Popay, J., (eds), Moving beyond effectiveness in evidence synthesis: methodological issues in synthesis of diverse sources of evidence. HAD: London.

Murray-Swank, A. B., Lucksted, A., Medoff, D. R., Yang, Y., Wohlheter, K., Dixon, L. B., (2006) Religiosity, Psychosocial Adjustment and subjective Burden of persons who care for those with mental illness. Psychiatric Service, March 2006, 57 (3).

Nachshen, J. S., & Miller, P. M., (2002) The family stress and coping interview for families of individuals with developmental disabilities: a lifespan perspective on family adjustment. Journal of Intellectual Disability Research, 47, pp 285-290.

NHS Executive (1999) Once a Day. London: HMSO.

NHS Performance Framework (2005) London: The Stationery Bookshop.

NHSCCA (1990) NHS & Community Care Act 1990, available online at < www.lukeclements.co.uk/resources-index/files/PDF%2010.pdf> Accessed 29 July 2012.

Nankervis, J.M. Bloch, S. Murphy, B.M. Herman, H. E. (1997) A classification of family carer's problems as described by counsellors. Journal of Family Studies, October 1997, 3(2), pp 169-182.

National Family Carer Network. Safeguarding Resources: Essential Guide. www.familycarers.org.uk

National Association of Social Workers (NASW) code of ethics (1994

Nottinghamshire Social Service Department in Becker, S., Becker, F., Silburn, R., Silburn, P., & Sempik, J., (2005) Carers Assessment in Nottinghamshire: Content, process and outcomes. Nottingham.

O'Brien (2012) The benefits and challenges of Kinship care. Child Care in Practice, April 2012, 18 (2), pp127 – 146.

Orsmond, G. I., & Seltzer, M. M., (2000) Brothers and sisters of adults with mental retardation: Gender nature of sibling relations. American Journal of Mental Retardation, 105 (6), pp 486 – 508.

Orsmond, G. I., & Seltzer, M. M., (2007) Siblings of individuals with autism or Down syndrome: effects on adult lives. Journal of Intellectual Disabilities Research, 51, pp 682 - 692.

Payne, G., & Payne, J., (2006) Key Concepts in Social Research. Sage: London.

Parmenter T. R., (2004) In Burton- Smith, R., McVilly, K.R., Yazbeck, M., Parmenter, T.R., Tsutsui, T., (2006) Service and support needs of Australian carers supporting a family member with disability at home. Journal of Intellectual and Developmental Disabilities: 2009, 34 (3), pp 239 – 247.

Pargament , K. I., Smith, B. W., Koenig, H. G., & Perez, L., (1997) Patterns of positive and negative religious coping with major life stressors. Journal of Scientific Study of Religion, Dec 1998, 37 (4), pp 710 – 724.

Patton, M. Q., (2002) In Guest, G., Bunce, A., Johnson, L., How many interviews are enough? An experiment with data saturation and variability. Field Methods Journal, 2006, 18 (1), pp 59 – 82.

Power, A. (2008) 'It's the system working for the system': carers' experiences of learning disability services in Ireland. Health and Social care in the Community, 17, 92-98.

Prosser, H., & Moss, S., (1996) Informal care networks for older adults with an intellectual disability. Journal of Applied Research in Intellectual Disabilities, 9 (1), pp 17 – 30.

Princess Royal Trust (2002) Keeley, B., & Clarke, M., (2002) Carers Speak out project report on findings and recommendations. London: Princess Royal Trust for Carers.

Quereshi, H., Patmore, C., Nicholas, E., and Bamford, C., (1998) Overview: Outcomes of Social Cares for older people and Carers. York: Social Policy Research Unit.

Rabinowitz, Y.G., Hartlaub, M.G., Saenz, E.C., Thompson, L.W., Gallanger- Thompson, D., (2009) Is religious coping associated with cumulative health Risk? An examination of religious coping styles and health behavior patterns in Alzheimer's dementia caregivers. Journal of religion and health, 2010, 4, pp 498 – 512.

Ramsden, S.,(2010) Practical Approaches to co-production: Building effective partnerships with people using services, carer, families and citizens. In Putting people first, 16 November 2010, Department of Health.

Rapp, C. A., and Goscha, R. J., (2006) Strengths Model: Case Management with people with psychiatric disabilities. Oxford: Oxford University Press.

Rawlings , A. J., (1988) In Deem, R., The future of educational research in the context of the social sciences: a special case. British Journal Of Educational Studies, 1996, 44 (2), pp 143 – 158.

Richards, L., & Morse, J. M (2007) Read me first for a user's guide to qualitative methods. (2nd ed). Sage: Thousand Oaks, CA.

Riesman, C., (1993) Narrative Analysis: Qualitative methods series no. 30. London: Sage.

Roberto, K. A., (1995) Family caregivers of aging adults with disabilities: a review of care giving literature. In: Roberto, K. A. (eds) The elderly Caregiver: caring for adults with developmental disabilities, pp 3 – 18. Newbury Park, CA: Sage Publications.

Robinson, C., & Williams, V., (2001) Carers of people with learning disabilities and their experience of 1995 Carers Act. BJSW, 2001, 32 (2), pp 169 -183.

Rooney R.H. & Rooney G.D (2002) in Hepworth D.H. , Rooney R.H. & Rooney G.D (2009) Direct Social work Practice: Theory and skills. Boston: Cengage Learning.

Rose, M., Rubin, A. E., Shelley, I., White-Means , N., (2009) Informal Care giving: Dilemmas of Sandwiched Caregivers. Journal of Family Economic Issues, 2009, 30, pp 2525-267.

Rubin, H., & Rubin, I., (1995) Qualitative Interview: a method to madness. Thousand Oaks, CA: Sage Publications

Rubin (2008) In Rubin, A., & Babbie, E. R., (2008) Research methods for social work. 6 th ed. Belmont, CA: Thomson Higher Education.

Rubin, A., & Babbie, E. R., (2008) Research methods for social work. 6 th ed. Belmont, CA: Thomson Higher Education.

Ryan, G. W., & Bernard, H. R., (2003) Techniques to identify themes. Field Methods Journal, Feb 2003, 15 (1), pp 85 – 109.

Saleebey, D., (2009) The strengths Perspective in social work Practice. Boston, MA: Pearson Education.

Savenye, W. C., & Robinson, R.S., (2005) Using qualitative research methods in higher Education. Journal of Computing in Higher Education, 2005, 16 (2), pp 65 – 95.

Savundranayagam, M.Y. et al (2011) A dimensional Analysis of caregiver burden among spouses and adult children. Gerontologist, 51(3), pp 321-331.

SCIE, In Needham, C., Carr, S., (2009) Research briefing 31: Co-production: an emerging evidence base for adult social care transformation. London Social Care Institute of Excellence.

SCIE, 2008, Having a break: good practice in short breaks for families needs and disabilities. London: Social Care Institute of Excellence.

Scourfield, P., (2005) Understanding why Carers Assessments do not always take place. Practice: Social Work in Action, 2005, 17 (1), pp 15 – 28.

Seddon, D., Robinson, C, Reeves, C., Tomms, Y., Woods, B., & Russell, I., (2006) Carers Assessment into practice. BJSW, 2007,

Seddon, D, & Harper, G., (2009) What works well in Community Care? Quality in Aging and Older Adults, 2009, 10 (4), pp 8 – 17.

Seltzer, M. M., Greenberg, J. S., Floyd, F. J., Pettee, Y., & Hong, J., (2001) Life course impacts of parenting a child with a disability. American Journal of Mental Retardation, 106, pp 265 – 286.

Selwyn, J., (2012) Sibling kinship carers in England: evidence from the 2001 UK population census. Children & Youth Services Review, Jan 2012, 34 (1), pp 194 - 199.

SEN In Lewis, A., (2004) And when did you last see your father? Exploring views of children with learning disabilities. British Journal of Special Education, March 2004, 31 (1), pp 3 – 9.

Shaw, I., (1999) 'Evidence for Practice', in Shaw, I., and Lishman, J, (eds) Evaluation and Social Work Practice. London. Sage.

Shaw, C., McNamara, R., Abrams, K., Canings-John, R., Hood, K., Longo, M., Myles, S., O'Mahony, S., Roe, B., Williams, K., (2009) Systematic review of respite care in frail adults. Health Technology Assessment Program, 2009, 13 (20).

Silverman, D. (2001) Interpreting Qualitative Data. 2nd ed. London: Sage.

Sloper, P., (2006) In Webb, R., Greco, V., Sloper, P., & Beecham, J., (2008) Key works and schools: meeting the needs of children and young people with disabilities. European Journal of Special Needs Education, 23, pp 189 – 205.

Social Care Institute for Excellence (SCIE) undated Website available at: http://www.scie.org.uk

Social Policy Research Unit, In Arksey, A., & Glendinning, C., (2007) Choice in the context of informal care-giving. York: University of York.

Stalker, K., (eds)(2003) Carers. Research Policy and Planning, 2003, 21 (2), pp 57 – 61.

Strauss, A., In Strauss, A., Corbin, J. M., (1990) Basics of Qualitative Research. Newbury Park, CA: Sage.

Smith, G.C., Hatfield, A. B., & Miller, D. C., (2000) Planning by older mothers for the future care of offspring with serious mental illness. Psychiatric Services, 51, pp 1162 – 1166.

Strozier, A. L., The effectiveness of support groups in increasing social support for kinship caregivers. Children & Youth Services Review, May 2012, 34(5), pp 876 -881.

Tait, D., & Genders, B., (2002) In Lin, J. D., Hsu, S.W., Yen, C. F., Chou, Y.T., Wu, C., Chu, C.M., Loh, C.,(2009)Role of general practitioners in the provision of healthcare services for people with intellectual disability: a national census in Taiwan. Journal of Applied Research in Intellectual Disability, Nov 2009, 22 (6), pp 582 – 591.

Taylor, P.C., Fraser, B.J., Fischer, D.L., (1995) in Monitoring constructivist classroom learning environments. International Journal of Educational Research, 1997, 27 (4), pp 293-302.

The British Psychological Society. 2011 Dementia and people with learning disabilities. Sept 2009. http://dcp-ld.bps.org.uk. Accessed 5 July 2012.

The Carers and Disabled children Act 2000, available online at < www.lukeclements.co.uk/resources-index/files/PDF%2010.pdf> Accessed 29 July 2012.

The Carers Equal Opportunity Act 2004, available online at < www.lukeclements.co.uk/resources-index/files/PDF%2010.pdf> Accessed 29 July 2012.

The Equality Act (2010) Available online at www.calerstones.nhs.uk/files/publications Accessed 27 July 2012

The Human Rights Act (1998) available online at < www.lukeclements.co.uk/resources-index/files/PDF%2010.pdf> Accessed 29 July 2012.

The Mental Capacity Act (2007) London: Office of Public Sector Information.

Treneman, M., Corkery, A., Downdney, L., Hammond, J., Respite care needs met and unmet: assessment of needs for children with disability. Developmental Medicine and Child Neurology, 1997, 39 (8), pp548 – 553.

Twigg, J., & Atkin, K., (1994) Carers perceive: Policy and practice in informal care. Buckingham & Philadelphia: Open University.

Thompson, N., (2006) Power and Empowerment: Theory into Practice. Lyme Regis, Dorset: Russell House Publishing.

Thomson, R., Bell, R., Holland, J., Henderson, S., McGrellis, S., and Sharpe, S., (2002) Critical Moments: Choice, Chance and Opportunity in Young People's Narrative of Transition. Sociology, 36 (2), pp335-354.

Van Excel, J., Moree, M., Koopmanschap, M., Schreuder, G., & Broywer, W., (2006) Respite Care: an exploratory study of demand and use in Dutch informal caregivers. Health Policy, 78, pp 194 – 208.

Van Excel, J., De Graaf, G. & Brouwer, W. (2008) Give me a break! Informal caregiver attitudes towards respite care. Science Direct Health Policy, 88, 73-87.

Wales, J., & Pryjmachuk, S., Mental Health care co-coordinators' perspectives on carers assessments. Mental Health Review Journal, Dec 2009, 14 (4), pp 46- 55.

Wardhaugh, J., & Wilding, P., (1993) In Cambridge, P., (1998) The Physical Abuse of people with learning disabilities and challenging behavior: lessons for commissioners and providers. Tizard Learning Disability Review, 1998, 3 (1), pp 18 - 26.

Watzlawick, P., (1967) In Watzlawick, P., Weakland, J. H., and Fish, R., (1974) Change: Principles of problem formulation and problem resolution. New York: WW Norton.

Weekes, L., (2008) In Halbach, N. S. J., Smeets, E. E. J., Chrander, S., Stumpel, C. T. R. M., VanSchrojenstein, H. H., Maasjkant, M. A., Curfs, L.M.G.,(2008) Aging in people with specific genetic syndromes: Rett Syndrome. American Journal of Medical Genetics, part A. August 2008; 146 (15), pp 1925 – 1932.

Weekes, L. E., Nilsson, T., Bryanton, O., and Kozma, A., (2008) Current and Future concerns of older parents of sons and daughters with intellectual disabilities. Journal of Policy and Practice in Intellectual Disabilities, Sept 2009, 6 (3), pp 180 -188.

Weisman, J. A., (1997) In Canda, E. R., Furman, L. D., (2009) Spiritual diversity in Social work practice: the heart of help. Oxford : Oxford University Press.

Welch, V., Hatton, C., Emerson, E., Robertson, J., Collins, M., Langer, S., Wells, E., (2012) Do short breaks and respite services for families with a disabled child in England make a difference to siblings? A qualitative analysis of sibling and parent responses. Children and Youth Service Review, Feb 2012, 34 (2), pp 451 -459.

WHO The ICD-10 Classification of mental and behavioral Disorders: Clinical Description and Diagnostic Guidelines. Geneva. WHO 1992.

Wiggs, L., & Stores, G., (1996) In Stores, G., (1999) Sleep disorders in children and adolescents. Journal of continuing professional development: Psychiatric Treatment.

Wiles, J. (2003) Daily geographies of caregivers: mobility routine, scale. Social science and medicine, 57,pp1307-1325.

Williams, U., Piamjariyakul, J Ca, Hafeman (2010) Developmental Disabilities: Effects on well siblings. Issues in comprehensive Pediatric Nursing, 2010, 33 (1).

Wilkie & Barr, O., (2008) Respite services for people who have an intellectual disability. Learning Disability Practice, 2009, 11 (5), pp 30- 36.

Wilson, K., Ruch, G., Lymbery, M., (2008) Social Work: An introduction to contemporary practice. Harlow, Essex: Pearson Education.

Wing, L., & Gould, B., (1979) In Wing, L., The definition and prevalence if autism: A review. European Child and Adolescent Psychiatry, 1993, 2 (1), pp 61 – 74.

Wing, L., (1981) Language, social and cognitive impairments in autism and severe mental retardation. Journal of Autism and Developmental Disorders, 1981, 11 (1), pp 31-44.

Wolcott , H. F., (1994) Transforming Qualitative Date: description, analysis and interpretation. London: Sage.

Woods, P., (2006) Qualitative Research. Available online at http://www.edu.plymouth.ac.uk/resined/qaul (Accessed 10 February 2012).

WHO In Foster, G. M., Behavioral science research: problems and prospects. Social Science and Medicine, 1987, 24 (9), pp 709 – 717.

Yeandle, S, Bennett, C., Buckner, L., Shipton, L., Suokos, A., (2006) Who cares wins: the social business benefits of supporting working carers. London: Carers UK.

Yoong, A., & Karitas, S., (2012) The impact of caring for adults with learning Disabilities on quality of life of parents. Journal of Intellectual Disability Research, June 2012, 56 (6), pp 609 – 619.

Young, A. F., Chesson, R.A., and Wilson, A. J. People with Learning disabilities, carers and care workers awareness of health risks and implications for primary care. Family Practice , 2007, 24 (6), pp 576-584.

Yueh-Chung, C., Chi, C., Li-Yeh, F., Health status, social support and quality of life among family carers of adults with profound intellectual and multiple disabilities (PIMD) in Taiwan. Journal of Intellectual & Developmental Disability, Mar 2011, 36 (1), pp 73-79.

APPENDIX A: The instrument   (The interview guide)

INTRODUCTION: ICE BREAKER. Issue information sheet and explain the research. Explain confidentiality, Explain recording, sign consent form. Ask bio-demographic details.

1. QUESTION: Can you tell me how you got to know about the Carers' Assessment? (probe) When were you assessed, by whom, Where?

2. QUESTION: Can you tell me about your experiences of having your needs assessed? (probe) How did you feel? Was the cared for present? What needs did you specify?

3. QUESTION: Can you tell me how a Carers Assessment has impacted on your life? (probe)

4. QUESTION: Can you explain how your needs were met after your assessment? (probe) How did you actually start accessing the services? Which services i.e. work/leisure/

education do you access? What did you have to do to get the services? How did the services meet your needs? How has this impacted your caring? Is there a gap in service provision? Are the services you wanted available for you?

5. QUESTION: Could you tell me about the services for carers in this borough? (probe)

6. QUESTION: What services are available for the person you care for in this borough? (probe)

7. QUESTION: Are there services for Carers you would like that are not available? (probe)

8. QUESTION: Do you have anything else to add?

ENDING. Stop recording. Ensure participant is not distressed. Reassure confidentiality.

APPENDIX B: Participant Consent form

CONSENT FORM

Title of the study: The Right to a Carer's Assessment: Exploring the Experiences of Carers of People with Learning Disabilities.

The research participant should complete the whole of this sheet himself.

Any questions should be directed to Shingi Sakuringwa (researcher/ student) at any point before, during and after the interview. Contact details withheld.

YES   NO

Have you read the Research Participant Information Sheet?

Have you had an opportunity to ask questions and discuss this study?

Have you received satisfactory answers to all your questions?

Do you understand that you will not be referred to by name in any report concerning the study?

Do you understand that you are free to withdraw from the study:

- At any time;
- Without having to give a reason for withdrawing; and
- Without affecting your future care.

I agree to my interview being recorded.

I agree to the use of non-attributable direct quotes when the study is written up or published.

Do you agree to take part in this study?

Signature of Research Participant:

Date:

Name in block letters:

Appendix C   INFORMATION SHEET
Research Participant Information Sheet

WANTED FOR A STUDY: CARERS OF PEOPLE WITH LEARNING DISABILITIES. I would like to invite you to take part in research. Before you decide to take part, I would like to tell you more about the research and your involvement.

1. Who am I?

I am Shingi Sakuringwa, a student currently doing the final year. For the purpose of my dissertation, I am conducting a study with carers of people with learning disabilities who had an assessment of their needs on the impact of having had a carer's assessment.

2. What is the purpose of the study?

The aim of the study is to explore the experiences of Carers of people with learning disabilities who have been assessed and are in receipt of services.

3. Why have you been invited to take part in this research?

You are invited to take part in this study because you are a Carer for a person with a learning disability. You should be able to talk comfortably about your experiences of the Carers' Assessment in English.

4. Do you have to take part in this study?

No. Participation is voluntary. Read through the leaflet. If you choose to participate, once the research has begun, you are free to stop taking part at any time without giving a reason. If you decide to take part, you will participate in a one hour face to face recorded interview to be conducted at a venue of your choice.

5. What are the risks of taking part in the research?

Some Carers might find taking part in the research distressing in discussing their experiences. Local counselling services, including those at the Carers Centre will be accessed to support Carers. If you decide to participate in the research, you may lose up to 1 hour to complete the interview.

6. What happens if you do not want to carry on with the study?

You can withdraw from the study at any time, without giving a reason. Any services you are currently receiving will not be affected whether or not you participate in the study.

7. What will happen to the results? Will your taking part be kept confidential?

It is hoped that the results will help professionals to get a better understanding of how to support Carers of people with learning difficulties. The comments you make during the interview will be anonymised in any publication. I may use quotes to tell people what you think but your real name will not be used. All data collected in this study will be treated as highly confidential. The confidentiality is limited as any disclosure of safeguarding issues will be explored and if necessary discussed with the Dissertation Supervisor and Manager of the Centre for further action to be taken.

At no time will your name be associated with any findings. Your identity will be protected when publishing the results but if needs be your consent will be sought. The information will be kept on a computer but no names will be put on the computer.

8. What if there is a problem or you have a complaint?

This research is not receiving any funding. The researcher is seeking Brunel University Ethics Committee Approval. If you have any concerns or complaints please contact the researcher or the supervisor on the contact details given below. Alternatively, please contact the Chair of the School Research ethics, details withheld.

I would be most grateful if you could contact me on (number withheld) if you wish to participate in this study.

SUPERVISOR

Please contact my Supervisor should you have complaints or need more information about this research. (Contact details withheld)

Appendix D   Consent from the Carers Centre

CARERS CENTRE LETTERHEAD

University Ethics Board

Dear Sir

This letter serves to confirm that we have given Shingi Sakuringwa permission to carry out research on the impact of a Carers Assessment on carers of people with a learning disability.

Yours faithfully

Appendix E   Transcript 03   CC 10.30am   26 June 2012

1.   QUESTION, SS: Can you tell me how you got to know about the Carers' Assessment?

SP: Well, that was in ..ah... , my son.... is 22 now.. he was 17... yes ..that was 2007 when he was going to college. His social worker came round to my house and we had a chat whilst she filled in the form. Staff at the Carers' Centre told us about carer's assessments and I requested one. The Centre made all the arrangements.

2.QUESTION: Can you tell me about your experiences of having your needs assessed?

SP: I felt good about social services enquiring about me and my needs. I felt they were interested in my needs and this raised my personal expectations. I thought I would get real help to manage. We are a big family, I have 5 children. ..... Is the fourth. I was able to talk about my caring role and how it impacts my life. Oh, the social worker was very patient, listening to me go on and on. My husband was there as well and we were able to express our needs as a family. My family is bi-racial. My husband is from … (African country).

SS: What needs did you identify for yourself and your husband?

SP: I would say separate needs. We both needed time to ourselves from the caring role, respite and to be able to have leisure time. I wanted to work, my husband already works.

SS: The government also gave you the right to access education, did you need that?

SP: I did but for many different short course, art, and knowledge about different conditions like autism, managing diabetes, obesity etc. I did not enrole for a college course; neither did I look for a job because they always called me at his college when they could not manage or if there were behavior problems. I don't think there is an employer who understands the need to rush off and deal with things, which sometimes at the family level, are easy, simply solved because of knowledge of bringing up a child or a sibling with learning disability. At a public level the care plan does not capture some of the nuances of the challenges faced by carers and the fact that different environments and approaches produce challenges for which family carers have inbuilt risk assessment procedures, but the public does not.

SS: So apart from having slightly separate needs from your husband, was there anything else in the actual assessment that you want to talk about?

SP: Yes, my husband has a proud culture where you are supposed to keep your family's business to yourself and not talk about your problems openly with outsiders. It is a kind of chin up approach. You deal with family problems as a family and manage your own business. I did more talking than he did at the assessment. I like to talk and request for help. I would say, I am more open to outside help than my husband is. He believes in the family being self sufficient. This is why now, my son is on Jobseekers Allowance not Employment support.

SS: Can you explain that, you said he is on DLA Medium rate for care and low for mobility. Shouldn't he be receiving ESA?

SP: …… is 6 foot 2 and weighs 28 stone. If he does not open his mouth, one won't know that he has a learning disability. He can do some tasks because we have both taught him. In college, he helps other students and towers over many people. He has done construction courses and can work with supervision. He is proud of working and will tell you quickly that he is good at putting things away such as carrying from a van onto shelves etc. My husband and I have agreed that he cannot be on ESA, just receiving money, he can work with supervision on a job which is appropriate for his skill level. He goes to the Job centre to sign on and he gets called for jobs. I see this as the influence from my husband for self reliance. It has brought …. happiness and sadness as well. He goes out of the home and meets many people, earns money but people's expectations of him out there have also caused great sadness.

SS: What has happened?

SP: He gets called for jobs and sometimes he is assigned work he can't do. Supervisors are not always there who understand that he has a learning disability and sometimes we have been called out when he does not understand what is happening and he displays challenging behavior.

3.QUESTION: Can you tell me how a Carers Assessment has impacted on your life?

SP: I can't say it has impacted my life because at the time of the assessment, my son was already in college, so I already had a few hours each day to do a few things I wanted to do. And the services that the assessment offers, I already could not work at the time of the assessment. What job can employ you when you can get called to your son's school anytime? Well, yes we managed to get respite maybe for 3 weeks but this did not come directly after the assessment but from an emergency much later. Within that respite, the respite centre calls you many times to manage one issue or other. A care plan fails to capture certain details which families have learned to deal with from the childhood of the person with learning disabilities; those same things become major disasters for outsiders/ the community to manage because they are scared of being held accountable. It is difficult for us to switch off our phone and not respond to the phone calls for ….'s wellbeing. We worried more when he was on respite. The only real respite we have is when we leave ….. with his siblings, with my family or my husband's family. We know he will be well looked after. They know how to manage behavior or create environments where the behavior does not manifest or how to divert the behavior and get the best out of and for ….. Besides, the Carers Centre was already supporting me to access respite through the carers break funds, relax with trips etc. The respite has been reduced from 28 to 21 days; is not easy to get and does not really give us respite as it makes us even more anxious. I would say that the CA did not make an impact on my life. My son applied for Housing Association and he shares a house with 2 other people who have a learning disability. This did not come as a result of my carer's assessment but his own assessment.

4.QUESTION: Can you explain how your needs were met after your assessment?

SP: Nothing happened after the assessment. Nobody called me about anything. I was already using services from the Carers Centre. I concluded that it was just a piece of paper filled in to meet a government policy but with little practical implications to me as a carer. My mother-in-law passed away in …(African country) in 2009, two years after my CA. We were making arrangements to go to … (African country) and we contacted the Carers Centre. Again they made arrangements by calling social services. The social worker visited me and made a care plan for respite care. In the end we left ….. at home with his siblings because there was no immediate place for respite and we went to the funeral. Later when we came back is when we had 3 week's local Authority respite. We had respite again the following year and then just decided that although it is a great concept it is more bother. We stopped because the amount of phone calls you get you might as well look after ..... yourself ,as it is less stressful.

SS: Would you say that there is a gap in service provision? Are the services you wanted available for you?

SP: In my family, we have ways of working together around .....'s needs and we use each family member's strengths to work with him. My husband supervises personal care, meal times and getting things done physically which ... can do. My sons do that as well as support with community access and fashion conscious shopping, games as well as computer games. My daughter is a listener. My other son plays the piano and sings. As a result when ...... spends time with each of us he has a different activity he is doing, including what he likes to do. This is how we have always been as a family so there has been no change on the caring role, we are able to share the caring. I worry about ..... and I go everywhere with him because I can read his communication. He lives in a Housing Association. I support him with budgeting but the rent and bills are high and sometime I use my own money for his groceries. He has had building construction training but he does great work at the special school with the younger children. He is there at the Day centre with other people with learning disabilities and most of them are 18 years old. His size makes him look even older than most of them. It is the same group he sees week after week. ...... likes to help others and so he keeps busy at the Day Centre. What I would have wanted government to do for me as a carer is to get me services such as ironing, laundry two times a week which really would give me a break during the week so I have more vitality to carry on. My family help but they all work so during the day, I am the one available for ..... because caring does not stop with independent living. It takes on a different dimension of supervision, extension of worry into the unknown which follows vulnerability linked to .....'s learning disability.

SS: So job wise, you think ..... would make a good assistant in such an almost predictable environment as a Day Centre?

SP: Yes, because most of what happens in the Day Centre or other such places there are things .... understands. He has gone for one job at ..... but the job description changed whilst he was there because of staff shortage. The supervisor did not realise that he cannot be at the till because he is unable to count and work out change. .....'s size makes members of the public assume that he is competent in many things. The environments become confusing for him. He did not understand why he was not assigned to packing shelves as promised; did not understand why the supervisor was angry and why customers were shouting. His challenging behavior brought the police who then called us. This never happens when .... is assigned work he can do. Such things make me very anxious. I am all for access to the community for people with learning disabilities but I am aware as a carer that the shifting community access environment presents challenges for people with learning disabilities and the public's perception of their employability. There is need to sensitise employers and the public. I have attended meetings with him to ensure that he understands things because we have to repeat things for him to understand. So, even when ….. is living independently, I worry about many things relating to his welfare and I am always 'on call'. The burden of care just shifts. Having …. live independently does not reduce my worrying or my care because I know what he is doing every day and can anticipate where challenges will occur.

SS: Government policy wants community access for people with learning disabilities though?

SP: Yes, but the community has expectations which some people with learning disabilities might not fulfill. My son, big as he is, the public expect him to be able to perform. When he cannot, they ask rhetorical questions like, ' Are you stupid or what ?' My son does not understand why he is being insulted because most of his life has been in environments which have shown him patience, nurturing and encouragement; when he was unable to do something at school or the Day Centre, he had comments like, ' Come on let's try it like this. / You hold this end and I will hold that end / …. take the spoon/ pen and try again.' So whilst government policy is meant for equality of opportunity, the public language is still not sensitive. What is perceived as public banter can result in challenging behavior and the public then question access to the community. I always find myself confronting such comments on his behalf.

5.QUESTION, SS: Could you tell me about the services for carers in this borough?

SP: I attend most of the services run by the Carers Centres which make it easier for carers to get into the cinema, theatre, museums, parks etc for free or for a smaller fee. There are also plenty of courses, short courses such as pottery, painting, and disease related courses, courses set up by the Carers Centres so that carers get to know about policy which affects them, personalisation and benefits changes. I now do volunteer work run by the council to assess environmental damage in the local area and I get invited to meetings for carers.

SS: You have a lot of information about issues of dignity, learning disabilities and policy.

SP: Yes, I have attended a lot of courses and sat in many meetings about care. You see, the employment programs are fine but there is no follow through to give an actual job. Most of what he does are casual jobs here and there and I end up using my own money to buy him grocery. The Housing Association is raising the rent. It is more difficult for my son to understand that he is receiving benefits but it is not enough to pay for basics.

6.QUESTION: What services are available for …..in this borough?

SP: ….is in Housing Association accommodation. He has a support worker who supports the 3 of them sharing the flat. …. gets support to use the gym and has occasional work.

He is a member of Mencap and does a lot of activities with them including disco, cinema and football. He goes to the Day Centre twice a week. He has done carpentry but there was only one apprenticeship given so continuity is lacking for the employment prospects. …. has free tickets to watch football matches at the stadium. He knows how to get home to his flat and from there how to use his free bus pass to get to our house, but if for some reason, the route is changed he gets confused. He calls one of the family to help him and gives his phone to the bus driver to explain where he is. Those are routines he follows for his own safety, but he is vulnerable. If he has to go anywhere else, we support him. My whole family has worked hard to train him to this level. I call him to ensure he is where he is meant to be. His size makes people assume a lot not knowing that psychologically he is 10 years old. ……'s siblings' children help him as well, so that learning disability which affected mine, my children's generation is being sensitised to the next generation. My grand children are all very protective of ..

7.QUESTION, SS: Are there services for Carers you would like that are not available?

SP: It is a case of what services were there that are no longer here because of the spending cuts. Centre XYZ has closed and those are centres that supported carers where you could talk to the staff about your issues and they would support you. The new centre that opened does not have facilities for carers to meet and interact with other carers. So services we have always relied on are being cut off and what replaces them does not meet my need to sit down and chat with staff, which sometimes is the only respite the carer has in between waiting for the Day centre pick up.

8.QUESTION, SS: Do you have anything else to add?

SP: I cannot think of anything, really. Just that when you are a carer, you are more than that because I am involved in the lives of all my five children but government has decided to link me only with one of them and label me with his support. We are a family, I am a wife, sister, daughter, aunt, etc. …..'s needs make us all in my family expend more time meeting his needs and supporting him. I meet ….'s needs, whilst also multi tasking to meet the needs of the whole family, and my own. I love all my children.

SS: Thank you very much for your time and your contribution to my research

Appendix F   Ethics approval
23 April 2012

Proposer: Shingi Sakuringwa

Title: Exploring the experiences of carers who have had an assessment and care for a person with learning disability

Reference: 12/3/SWK/07

LETTER OF APPROVAL

The School Research Ethics Committee has considered the amendments recently submitted by you in response to the Committee's earlier review of the above application.

The Chair, acting under delegated authority, is satisfied that the amendments accord with the decision of the Committee and has agreed that there is no objection on ethical grounds to the proposed study. Approval is given on the understanding that the conditions of approval set out below are followed:

- The agreed protocol must be followed. Any changes to the protocol will require prior approval from the Committee.

Please note that:

- Research Participant Information Sheets and (where relevant) flyers, posters, and consent forms should include a clear statement that research ethics approval has been obtained from the School of Health Sciences and Social Care Research Ethics Committee.

- The Research Participant Information Sheets should include a clear statement that queries should be directed, in the first instance, to the Supervisor (where relevant), or the researcher. Complaints, on the other hand, should be directed, in the first instance, to the Chair of the School Research Ethics Committee

- Approval to proceed with the study is granted subject to receipt by the Committee of satisfactory responses to any conditions that may appear above, in addition to any subsequent changes to the protocol.

- The School Research Ethics Committee reserves the right to sample and review documentation, including raw data, relevant to the study.

(Name withheld)

Research Ethics Committee Officer

School of Health Sciences and Social Care

23 April 2012

Proposer: Shingi Sakuringwa

Title: Right to a Carer's Assessment: Exploring the Experiences of Carers of People with Learning Disabilities.

Reference: 12/3/SWK/07

LETTER OF APPROVAL

The School Research Ethics Committee has considered the amendments recently submitted by you in response to the Committee's earlier review of the above application.

The Chair, acting under delegated authority, is satisfied that the amendments accord with the decision of the Committee and has agreed that there is no objection on ethical grounds to the proposed study. Approval is given on the understanding that the conditions of approval set out below are followed:

- The agreed protocol must be followed. Any changes to the protocol will require prior approval from the Committee.

Please note that:

- Research Participant Information Sheets and (where relevant) flyers, posters, and consent forms should include a clear statement that research ethics approval has been obtained from the School of Health Sciences and Social Care Research Ethics Committee.

- The Research Participant Information Sheets should include a clear statement that queries should be directed, in the first instance, to the Supervisor (where relevant), or the researcher. Complaints, on the other hand, should be directed, in the first instance, to the Chair of the School Research Ethics Committee

- Approval to proceed with the study is granted subject to receipt by the Committee of satisfactory responses to any conditions that may appear above, in addition to any subsequent changes to the protocol.

☐ The School Research Ethics Committee reserves the right to sample and review documentation, including raw data, relevant to the study.

Name Withheld

Research Ethics Committee Officer

School of Health Sciences and Social Care

Appendix G   Colour coded Transcript
Transcript 02   CC 11 am   18 June 2012

(Words in Capitals are CODES IDENTIFIED)

1.QUESTION, SS: Can you tell me how you got to know about the Carers' Assessment?

M.R: Well, I had come to the Carers Centre, in 2005 for relaxation. The staff made a REFERRAL to Social Services and a social worker visited me at home to do the assessment. They also did a benefits check for my son. Sub-theme; Assessment process.

2.QUESTION, SS: Can you tell me about your experiences of having your needs assessed?

M.R: We had a nice chat actually, talking about me, how I was coping with the care for my son, ... He is 38. I enjoyed the chat. I think she stayed for almost an hour. My friend, who is also a carer, had taken my son to the shops. I felt that I mattered as a carer and that they were not just focussing on my son only. Sub-theme; Assessment experience.

SS: What needs did you specify?

M.R: She said I can go to college or work, at my age, I am not going to do that! Besides, caring for …. keeps me busy. I do not have time for the services government is offering. Sub-theme: Services from CA

SS: You are also entitled to respite, did you not need that?

M.R: What respite? That would cause worry for me?(RESPITE WORRY) When I go on holiday, which I do to (Caribbean country) , I go with ….. Then my family, from my side and my late husband's side will support ….. and I can actually rest(Sub-theme; Worry with community access), girl. I have gone twice since becoming a member of this Carers Centre because the staff support me with grant applications for holidays.

3.QUESTION, SS: Can you tell me how a Carers Assessment has impacted your life?

M.R: For me personally, I don't think it did a lot. My son was re-housed for some time in a Housing Association flat, sharing with two other people who also have a learning disability. This happened as a result of his benefits reassessment and maybe as a result of my needs assessment because I explained that I have very little time to myself. At that time, my husband was alive. (Sub-theme; Assessment impact) We had to do budgeting for him. It worked for a while, then my husband was hospitalised. That was a very stressful time for all of us as he was in and out of hospital for more than six months. He died at home.(JUGGLING MANY THNGS)

SILENCE….

SS: I am sorry about that.

SILENCE…

SS: Are you alright?

M.R: … I am alright really. I dealt with relatives in (Caribbean country) who wanted to reap where they never sowed. I told them, I was the man's wife and was not going to tolerate nonsense! (Smiles) (Sub-theme; Multi-role of the carer)

SS: How did …… take his dad's death?

M.R: He was fine then. But developed MENTAL HEALTH issues thereafter.

SS: What mental health problems is he presenting?

M.R: Well, he keeps loads of things, some he buys them and keeps them in huge piles. He is always piling things and he gets angry easily with a lot of mood swings.

SS: Hoarding?

M.R: Yes, that's the word. I have seen it on TV? ….. keeps clothes, game etc. At first they were under his bed and I asked him to move them. He put them in the cupboards for an afternoon. By the following morning, there were huge piles on the floor in his bedroom. I have tried to work with him to make order in his room but he gets very angry. He occasionally piles all my stuff everywhere in my bedroom as well. I have told him that I do not like that. He apologises, helps me to put it away and soon does it again. He apologises and says he does not want to make me sad.

SS: Have you talked to him about this and taken him to see specialists?

M.R: We talked. My son says, 'Dad died, what am I going to do when you die as well? Who will look after me?' I have reassured him but it is not enough. (Sub-theme; Challenging behavior) I have reassured him that his brother and sister-in-law, who live in London and support him often, will be there for him. My FAMILY in (Caribbean country) will SUPPORT him. I think he knows that I support him unconditionally, I can read his face and his movements and I know what he is saying even without speech. I know when he has had a nice day out and good interaction with the personal assistant even before he says anything. I worry about him hoarding. What medicine can cure that? I have taken him to psychiatrists. Sometimes he is fine for a few months then he starts piling things again.

SS: How do you manage all this?

M.R: I have taken him to specialists and learned about managing hoarding. He has a personal budget and once or twice a week, I employ an agency personal assistant to take him into the community either to watch a football game, go shopping or something. I also go to all the trips organised by the Carers Centre and come for the Carers relaxation day to take a break.(LEISURE) I really need the massages. I go to CHURCH because this helps me to accept my caring role.(Sub-Theme; Coping strategy with religion and leisure activities)

SS: What Activities do you do with your son?

M.R: Gardening, cooking, tiding up in the house. I have to supervise him because he can't do many things, so I do them with him. Oh, there is the day I asked him to watch the chips I was making for his lunch. Oh, girl, I laugh but it is not funny! I only went to the garden for a few minutes to take in the laundry, the pan almost caught fire, girl! (Laughs loudly) The chips got burned and he was sitting watching TV in the lounge. He can do his own personal care and dress himself with supervision. I can leave him in one part of the house by himself for an hour or so once he is dressed and has had a meal. He likes to watch TV or play TV games. It is a lot of work which requires me to be alert all the time. But by God's grace, I manage. Except for my painful joints, I am healthy, touch wood! (Sub-Theme; CARER HEALTH)

SS: Is religion a big part of your life and did you talk to the social worker about your religion?

M.R: It is and has always been from when I was little. It helped me to understand that some things I can't change them but have to live and manage my life. In my assessment, we did not talk about religion. I go to church and sometimes my son comes with me. In fact some of my church members take him for a few hours or go with him to church functions during the week. Most of them know him and I don't worry when they go with him because they understand how he is and encourage him to participate in whatever they do. That's why I was saying I did not need respite services. I am sure government respite will be for a longer time, but the carers at respite do not know my son as well as my friends at the church do, although they will have a care plan. It would just make me worry so much about how he is managing. (Sub-Theme; value of religion as a network and avenue for care sharing)

SS: I thought you said (your son) went into supported living, how come he lives with you now?

M.R: Girl, he was thin as a rack after eight months of living by himself. He can't cook, so he was ordering take out. Two months after he moved out of our home, his dad was admitted into hospital. Because of the stress of the next six months when I could not pay him attention, he got into debt, he lost a lot of weight. He moved back home about two weeks before his dad died.(Sub-theme; WEIGTHLOSS/ DEBT as part of living in the community)

4.QUESTION, SS: Would you say, then that the Carers Assessment met your needs after your assessment?

M.R: Not me directly but my assessment and his reassessment for his benefits and personal budget gave us a personal assistant which makes it easier for me to leave him for longer periods to go on trips and explore London or other areas. I do not want to go to college, or to work and my leisure is mostly associated with the activities of the Carers Centre or when I go to my country of origin. No social worker contacted me about the assessment afterwards. So although it made me feel good to be assessed, there was no follow up from social services, although they referred me to the Carers Centre.(Sub-theme; Assessment impact)

SS: How has this impacted your caring?

M.R: I have the personal budget for my son to go to the gym with his assistant, cinema, sports etc. So indirectly I benefit from time to myself and this makes dealing with some of the challenging issues easier to handle. .(Sub-theme; Assessment impact)

SS: Is there a gap in service provision as in are there services you feel you should have been included in your assessment?

M.R: I just wish there was a follow up from social services. I think my assessment form is just filed away without any feedback. (Sub-theme; Assessment process).

5.QUESTION, SS: Could you tell me about the services for carers in this borough?

M.R:I have followed up subsidised courses for flower arrangement, pottery, baking etc in the borough run by charity organisations. The museum has free or subsidised specials for carers and so do the threatres. There are several Carers Centres in the borough and no win no fee lawyers. I know many who use the free English lessons at the library. The Carers Centre has left leaflets in GP surgeries and pharmacies so as to reach more carers who are not accessing services. There are SHORT COURSES in budgets, benefits, art, craft, managing various conditions like diabetes, challenging behaviour, relaxation etc. (Sub-theme; short courses) Recently we had the twentieth anniversary of one Carers Centre and a lot of carers attend. There are a lot of services for carers.

6.QUESTION, SS: What services are available for your son in this borough?

M.R: The gyms have special programs including those related to balanced diet, the nearby stadium allows them in for free to watch matches, there are employment opportunities for people with learning disabilities. My son cannot work because he would find it difficult to follow instructions. There are companies which buy computer equipment for people with learning disabilities and there are special rates for cinemas.

7.QUESTION, SS: Are there services for Carers you would like that are not available?

MR:I can't think of anything.

8.QUESTION, SS: Do you have anything else to add?

M.R: Yes, that it is hard to look after someone with learning difficulties. My hopes were raised when I was assessed. For us to be ASSESSED AND NOT RECEIVE FEEDBACK it's not nice. (Sub-theme; Assessment process).

Appendix H (a) Thematic data reduction
TABLE A

Code   Number of participants who raised the issue

Challenging behaviour   8

Employment of people with LD   1

Mental health of people with LD   2

Community access; obesity/ weight loss

debt   8

Multi role of carers   10

Respite with family is best   6

Faith   8

Referral   10

Positive impact of CA   6

No feedback from social services   6

Good assessment experience   10

leisure   10

Short courses   10

Education   1

Working   4

Care sharing   8

Carer's health problems 5

Issues with the name 'carer'   2

(b)   Code Threading into major themes
Fourteen sub-themes were threaded into five major themes which are highlighted below in black.

Sub-themes assessment process (referral), assessment experience and Assessment impact have the common thread of carers narrating their perspectives of the CA. A major theme linking all three was Telling their story.

Subthemes; services from a carers assessment i.e. work, education, leisure and short courses, are part of Carer Self-development although leisure was also a major a coping strategy.

Postponement in dealing with carers' health issues or arranging appointments around caring, the many relationships and multi-roles in the carers' lives and challenging behavior raised the concept that carers put their life on hold to deal with caring.

Sub-themes; leisure, religion, care sharing with neighbours,/relatives/ friends/ faith based communities all shared the concept of carer's coping strategies.

Sub-themes; worry with community access, weightloss/ obesity / debt as part of living in the community, employment, the name carer , respite shared a running thread dealing with formal services.

TABLES of results

Table 3: Assessment process

Participant

1   CC Staff made.. arrangements and a social worker came to my house..... social worker .. referred me to ..CC.

2   .. the CC.....staff made a referral to Social Services and a social worker visited me at home to do the CA..... I just wish there was a follow up from social services. I think my CA form is just filed away without any feedback. .....My hopes were raised when I was assessed. For us to be assessed and not receive any feedback it's not nice.

3   His social worker came round to my house and we had a chat whilst she filled in the form. Staff at the CC told us about CA and I had requested one.

4   The teachers ….talked about an assessment of my needs. The head teacher called social services and an appointment was made….The social worker came to my house

5   My mother … died …. I became a fulltime carer then. My assessment…..a few months after ..funeral. My sister's social worker ….told me about the assessment.

6   .. my GP made a referral…. The social worker, who already knew my family came to my house to do the CA ..

7   ……CC,…. referred me to social services…. The social worker paid a visit to my house. …

8   …the head teacher told me about it and arranged it. The social worker came to my house to do the CA….

9   My late wife was the primary carer ,…. After the funeral, I had an assessment … I had just retired from teaching then and … I became the primary carer then. The social …told me about a CA

10   My mum .. was the primary carer for my sister, … She is now old and frail and I took over as the primary carer. … the social worker talked to us as a family and I chose to care for my sister. …. I was assessed by social worker …….

Table 4: Assessment experience

Participant

1   It was nice to talk about me and what I wanted. I felt special. I felt that government recognises the amount of work carers do.

2   We had a nice chat actually, talking about me, how I was coping….. I think she stayed for almost an hour…. I felt that I mattered as a carer.

3   I felt good about social services enquiring about me and my needs. I felt they were interested in my needs and this raised my personal expectations. I thought I would get real help to manage. I was able to talk about my caring role and how it impacts my life. Oh, the social worker was very patient, listening to me go on and on. My husband was there as well…

4   … we had a lovely chat over a cup of tea. My husband was there but he did not contribute much to the chat except to answer a few questions or nod in agreement. It was good to talk to someone about my role and explain the problems I have.

5   It was a chat and she filled in a form and asked about how I was managing and what I wanted to do. … I spoke mostly about how I was adjusting and the social worker was very helpful. I really appreciated her listening to me.

6   . I was able to talk about my caring role and what I want to do. It felt good to talk about my role as a carer......

7   It was lovely actually. Oh I talked and talked. The social worker was very patient and listened to me going on and on and she filled in a form. I felt good afterwards.

8   It was lovely actually, I must have talked for England. I enjoyed being able to talk about my caring and how it affects me. She filled in a form.

9   The social worker filled in a form and asked about how caring was affecting me. To be honest, so much had happened at the time that I cannot remember most of the actual assessment but we talked about me.

10   It was a nice chat actually. My sister was there. I talked about my caring role and how it affects me. I liked talking about it; it made me feel that I mattered.

Table 5: Assessment Impact

Participant   Assessment impact

1   I have a 23 year old son who has LD, a 5 year old son and a 3 year old daughter, I am busy. Nothing happened after the assessment. .... I don't think that the assessment services on offer met any of my personal needs. The government is offering work, education and leisure for carers but all that is not relevant to my life even now.

2   Besides, caring for my son keeps me busy. I do not have time for most of the services government is offering..........Not me directly but my assessment and his reassessment for his benefits and personal budget gave us a personal assistant which makes it easier for me to leave him for longer periods to go on trips and explore London or other areas. ... So indirectly I benefit from a little time to myself and this makes dealing with some of the challenging issues easier to handle.

3   Nothing happened after the assessment. ... I concluded that it was just a piece of paper filled in to meet a government policy but with little practical implications to me as a carer....The generic services; education and work do not meet my needs because I have to consider the impact on every member of my family.

4   I have done short two hour courses ... Those are relevant to my life and fit in the short amount of time I have when my son is in school...... Well, we were offered respite and a care plan was made for that......the social work referred me to this CC.... I accessed relaxation .... I have made more friends among the carers ... My life has a bit more quality to it although it is still very busy...

5   I would say the CA enabled me to lead a quality life as a carer. I was referred to the CC

6   Almost immediately after my CA....... I got time to distress and sleep. I use that time to sometimes attend CC activities although I cannot stay for long. I go shopping or meet friends. I have that relaxation time although it is short.

7   Some Wednesdays I attend the CC activities when my eldest daughter can stay with ….

8   Well, I was referred to the CC where I got support from other carers. I have made friends. I attend all the Relaxation days to have a massage and do the activities. …I have a job I do 3 times a week for 5 hours a day whilst my son is at school.

9   I receive Direct Payments for my son, … I still go into the school as a teaching assistant volunteer every morning, that helps me to cope with caring. …….   I was referred to the CC which I attend every Wednesday after school… ……. Well, in my retirement, I enjoy the short training courses on different topics..

10   Yes, the CA has improved my life as a carer.... I would say that assessment gave me my own life back in being able to go out and work with other people and being self fulfilled and having my own life. I interact with other carers and I come home a better carer.

Table 6: Leisure

Participant   Sub-theme: Leisure

1   I take the 3 year old and the 5 year old to school, I come back to deal with (my son's) self care. ……as for leisure, if I get 10 minutes to sit down with a cup of tea, that's leisure.

2   …my leisure is mostly associated with the activities of the CC.

3   I attend most of the services run by the CC which make it easier for carers to get into the cinema, theatre, museums, parks etc for free or for a smaller fee.

4   …the social worker referred me to this CC….. I accessed relaxation …. I have made more friends among the carers and I feel I can share and get support.

5   I am able to carry on most of the activities I used to do, going to the pub, and walking…… I attend activities at the CC….I can talk to the other carers. We have a support group for male carers…… I also have dancing and indoor games at another CC and dancing at … centre. … Yes, my needs in my retirement are met although I am busier because of caring.

6   …my son goes to a special school …   My daughter goes to a different school. I get to sleep during part of the day because my son sleeps maybe 4 hours in the night. . …

I could do with .. leisure but when do I take it? My mother is in London but she is elderly and sick herself. My partner does not help.

7   My four other children…..help me to get frequent breaks to meet friends, shop etc.

8   ..For me, just knowing that every Wednesday, I can go to the CC to meet other people is a break from my routine….. to have adult company. ……. .

9   I was referred to the CC which I attend every Wednesday after school. I have massage and I attend some training courses.

10   Once a week I come to the CC for relaxation and meeting other carers …I enjoy the trips I take and learn new things. …I come home a better carer.

Table 7: Education

Participant   Sub-theme   Education
1   The government is offering… education … but ..that is not relevant to my life even now. I don't want to learn anything,…. as there are no hours (in the day for me to do that).

2   I do not want to go to college…

3.   I did not enroll for a college course ….because they always call me at his college when they cannot manage or if there were behavior problems.

4.   My son's school calls me almost daily with one issue or other mostly to do with challenging behavior and on several occasions, I have to go to the school to attend to the issue…. my husband works full time. … my son does not easily accept strangers…. Where do I get time to work or go to college?

5   I am 71 years old now and …(my sister).. is 74 years old. I was 68 when I had my CA and had already retired from work. I did not want to work nor go to college. My caring role is demanding. So I asked for respite and time to myself.

6   …he goes to a special school and has challenging behaviour on the bus. When he gets to school they call every week about something or other. My daughter goes to a different school. I get to sleep during part of the day because my son sleeps maybe 4 hours in the night. I have to pick up my daughter at midday. Which course can I do in that period of time?

7   I don't want to start college at this age.

8   I do short training courses so that I keep up to date with his learning disability issues.

9   Well, in my retirement, I enjoy the short training courses on different topics at the CC and being able to volunteer at my school.

10   Well, I have done a teaching assistant course and have just completed it.

.. I chose to go to college, work and respite. … I was referred to the CC where they applied for an educational grant to pay my fees and I enrolled for the home training course.

Table 8: Short Courses

Participant

1   I was referred by the CC and attended free English lessons at the local library.

2   I have followed up subsidised courses for flower arrangement, pottery, baking etc in the borough run by charity organisation…. training in budgets, benefits, art, craft, managing various conditions like diabetes, challenging behavior…

3   I did ….many different short course, art, and knowledge about different conditions like autism, managing diabetes, obesity etc…. I have attended a lot of courses and sat in many meetings about care.

4   I have done short two hour courses at the CC about managing diabetes, managing challenging behavior, benefit changes etc. Those are relevant to my life and fit in the short amount of time I have when my son is in school.

5   We have a support group for male carers. There are only 7 of us in the group but we meet every two months in the evening at the centre because a few of them work. … there is always someone invited to speak to use about benefit changes, health issues or caring.

6   ..At 4 years old is when my son showed high level of activity, kicking, punching, vomiting, spitting and smearing faeces when he could. To be told that as a carer you can……have courses becomes almost irrelevant to me as a parent. …. Right now he goes to a special school and has challenging behaviour on the bus. When he gets to school they call every week about something or other. My daughter goes to a different school. …. What services the CA is offering me are irrelevant to my current circumstances…

7   I was able to do driving lessons from a carer's grant but that is open to all carers.

8   I have to pick up my son after school that why I can only attend short trips and short courses

9   I did not want to go to college.

10   Once a week I come to the CC …. and attending any short courses they have. I applied for a grant through the CC to do driving so I am able to transport my mum and sister around.

Table 9: Work

Participant   Sub-theme Work

1   ..all that is not relevant to my life even now. I…. cannot work as there are no hours I can work.

2   I do not want …to work.

3   … neither did I look for a job because they always called me at his college when they could not manage or if there were behavior problems I now do volunteer work run by the council to assess environmental damage in the local area and I get invited to meetings for carers.

4   Where do I get time to work?

5   I am 71 years old now and (my sister) is 74 years old. I was 68 when I had my carer's assessment and had already retired from work. I did not want to work….

6   .. So, which job can I do in that time? …. What services the CA is offering me are irrelevant to my current circumstances.

7   I don't want to work….at this age. If they had offered something that I could do for short periods in a day, I would probably do it.

8   I have a job I do 3 times a week for 5 hours a day whilst my son is at school.

9   I receive Direct Payments for …, so that I still go into the school as a teaching assistant volunteer every morning that helps me to cope with caring. I have also always enjoyed being around young people in school.

10   I got a job in a school where I used to be a volunteer. …working takes me out of the house for half a day four times a week and I am able to do my assignments and release the personal assistant at 3 pm when I take over as carer.

Table 10: Carers' Health

Participant   Sub-theme Carers' health

1   You can see the extra support I have on my arm and hand! I have shoulder problems and have had two operations on the shoulder. I have painful joints and high blood pressure.

2   It is a lot of work which requires me to be alert all the time…..and except for my painful joints, I am healthy,

3   Not discussed

4   ……..On Thursdays, my son goes to school as usual and then goes to football from 3 to 6 pm. So, that is my day to relax. I go shopping, do my hair, meet my friends and cook. I even had my operation on a Thursday. It was a minor operation. The doctor said I shouldn't do any work. Who would do it, I ask? … (Laughs)… I ended going back into hospital 2 days later because of course I had done work at home. Now I have joint problems and hypertension.

5   I have use of one arm because of polio and my joints are now a problem but I can still walk and need to exercise my legs.

6   ..My GP made a referral because I was always so tired.

7   Not discussed

8   Not discussed

9   Not discussed

10   Not discussed

Table 11: Multi role of the carer
Participant   Multi role of the carer

1   I take the 3 year old and the 5 year old to school, I come back to deal with my eldest son's self care. Then I have to go back at noon to collect the three year old and prepare lunch. I go back at 3 pm to pick up the 5 year old from school. …I am a mother to three children so my life is not just about being a carer for my son who has a learning disability. I do not identify myself as a carer only, which I feel the government does, … To me the word carer, means they are attaching me only to (my eldest son) and forgetting about my other relationships and about what else I want to do. All my children are valuable to me so I do not identify with a label which attaches me to one child only.

2   … then my husband was hospitalised. That was a very stressful time for all of us as he was in and out of hospital for more than six months. Then he died…. I do Gardening, cooking, tidying up in the house.

3   … My whole family has worked hard to train him to this level. …my son's siblings' children help him as well, so that learning disability which affected mine, my children's generation is being sensitised to the next generation. ………when you are a carer, you are more than that because I am involved in the lives of all my five children but government has decided to link me only with one of them and label me with his support. …. I meet .(my son's)… needs, whilst also multi tasking to meet the needs of the whole family, and my own.

4   My son's school calls me almost daily with one issue or other mostly to do with challenging behavior and on several occasions, I have to go to the school to attend to the issue. I am the primary carer for my son and my husband works full time. … my son does not easily accept strangers….

5   .. referred to the CC…this has extended my friendships. ….. We have a support group for male carers. There are only 7 of us in the group but we meet every two months in the evening at the centre because a few of them work. … It makes it easier for me to go back to my caring role. I also have dancing and indoor games at another CC and dancing at the…..centre. I belong to a walking club. … Yes, my needs in my retirement are met although I am busier because of caring.

6   …has challenging behaviour…. school ..they call every week about something or other. My daughter goes to a different school. I get to sleep during part of the day because …. sleeps maybe 4 hours in the night. I have to pick up my daughter at midday. . … My mother is in London but she is elderly and sick herself. My partner does not help.

7   …every Wednesday, I can go to the CC to meet others.. then pick him up from school afterwards…..

8   (The cared-for).. does not like to go out in public or to speak to those she does not know. I am the main carer.

9   … I had just retired from teaching then and that's when my wife passed on and I became the primary carer then.. I still have the house chores to do but I clean when I can.

10   I got a job in a school ………. I am able to transport my mum and sister around….. I work … for half a day four times a week and I am able to do my assignments and release the personal assistant at 3 pm when I take over as carer.

Table12: Challenging Behavior
Participant   Sub-theme; Challenging behavior

1   ..difficult times when I do not understand what ….. wants, he can't speak.. uses simple signs in pictures which we have laminated. Sometimes those signs are not

adequate or his medication does not seem to be taking effect of calming him down. ...... gets frustrated and agitated sometimes. Then I do not know what to do and even if I want to call someone, I don't know what to say is wrong. You also can not get an appointment quickly.

2   (How did ..... take his dad's death?) He was fine then. But developed mental health issues thereafter. ...Well, he keeps loads of things, some he buys them and keeps them in huge piles. He is always piling things and he gets angry easily with a lot of mood swings... .... says, 'Dad died, what am I going to do when you die as well? Who will look after me?' I have reassured him but it is not enough. ....

3   ...My son's size makes members of the public assume that he is competent in many things. The environments become confusing for him and he did not understand why he was not assigned to packing shelves as promised, did not understand why the supervisor was angry and why customers were shouting. His challenging behavior brought the police, who then called us. This never happens when (he) is assigned work that he is able to do. ... ...So whilst government policy is meant for equality of opportunity, the public banter is not sensitive. What is perceived as public banter can result in challenging behavior and the public then question some of the implications of access to the community. I always find myself confronting such comments on his behalf.

4   ..... has little speech and he only says the basic words necessary for what he wants only. ..... does not watch TV except the football matches. He does not like to interact with many people and certainly not strangers. When he is at home, he sits in his room, he likes sitting in the dark. We have tried changing that but it brings challenging behavior. Even his curtains are dark. ...... If you try to draw him out when he is not ready to let you into his world, he can become challenging, even breaking things.

5   I do not think so because for learning disability with my sister, it's is about services that she can do which do not bring challenging behavior.

6   .. son showed high level of activity, kicking, punching, vomiting, spitting and smearing feaces when he could. ...

7   Not discussed

8   ....has no speech and has difficulty interacting. At school, he has 1:1 support to read, play etc as he has a very short attention span. He can look at pictures but loses interest quickly. He works best with familiar people which is why I always ask the agency for the same personal assistant. He has poor fine motor skills. He finds it difficult to play with other children and has violent outbursts......

9   Not discussed

10   Not discussed

Table 13: Care Sharing

Participant   Sub-theme: Care sharing

1   My ex husband took the children to school and took ... out so I was able to talk without disruption.

2   When I go on holiday, which I do to (Caribbean country), I go with …. Then my family, from my side and my late husband's side will support ….. and I can actually rest, girl.

3   In my family, we have ways of working together around his needs and we use each family member's strengths to work with him. ….My son's siblings' children help him as well, so that learning disability which affected mine, my children's generation is being sensitised to the next generation. My grand children are all very protective of him

4   I have learned to study his body language and I know when to do things and when to let him be. My husband tends to do personal care and to play football with him and I do the rest.

5   I used to help mum especially when she was taking breaks to go to …(EU nation), I used to look after …. for short periods. My older sister, … is 79 and lives in(place in England), used to look after …. but she has health issues. Her daughter helps me if I want to take respite.

6   I get to sleep during part of the day because (my son) sleeps maybe 4 hours in the night.

7   My eldest daughter took her to the garden whilst I had my assessment. I have my four other children to help me although they all work and live in different parts of the city. My ex husband does not help although he lives in …..

8   I am now a lone parent since my son was 3 years old. When I really need help my ex husband steps in to help once in a while. …. During the weekend, his dad takes him to the football games or outings

9   We had two sons. The eldest lives in (EU Nation) with his family, so here, I am by myself. … finds it hard to interact socially. … I do not want to leave him with strangers but would love to go to (European country of origin) on holiday and see the rest of my family. The last time I went was before my wife died. Our eldest son stayed with him for two weeks. .

10   My mother had just me and my sister,…... Our dad past away about 13 years ago …… My mother is there but is too frail.

Table 14: Religion

Participant   Sub-theme; Religion

1   I thank God that I am able to cope….. Yes, it is a very important part. I have learned through faith to deal with learning disability, to be able to cope without cracking up, to deal calmly with challenging behavior. …..My faith carries me through difficult times…. No, the topic did not come up during the assessment.

2   I go to church because this helps me to accept my caring role……(religion is important).. It is and has always been from when I was little. It helped me to understand that some things I can't change them but have to live and manage my life. In my assessment, we did not talk about religion. I go to church and sometimes (my son) comes with me. …

3   We attend church together… We did not discuss religion during assessment but it is a very big part of our coping as a family. We have support from the church.

4   But God is good, he has helped me to cope…..I wouldn't be able to do all I do without God. I have always gone to church since I was a child. When I had my son I learned to depend on the grace of God to manage my caring role….

5   .. I resorted to the church and employed another church member.. (my sister)… knew ..(Did you have to go to church because ..(your sister).. used to go with your mum?) NO, I was an altar boy in my youth. We are Catholics. I have always gone to church. I found it helpful as I was growing up with a sibling with learning disabilities. Also some of the ladies bring cakes etc and we have tea afterwards. They invite her to choir practice as well and we use the taxi to get her there. This is what the church community does for her and it gives me a break as well.

6   Not discussed

7   I go to church every Sunday but she doesn't come with me. Oh it's a big part of coping with what I cannot change in my life. I have always gone to church any way. I felt that it helps me to come back home and be a better carer. No, the social worker was filling in a form as I talked, we did not discuss my religion.

8   Not discussed

9   Prayer is a very important part of my life. I take my son for mass every week…… I don't remember a lot of what we discussed (in the assessment) but I know we did not talk about that. It never came up

10 I would not be able to cope without it…… the social worker was filling in a form and that topic did not come up. I have always gone to church. It helps me to deal with the difficult things in life.

Table 15: Respite

Participant THEME: Respite

1 .. The phone calls from the respite centre started enquiring about all sorts. …On the other hand I have gone on holiday with the whole family from the grants the CC supported me to get. We went to (European country of origin) on holiday to my mother's. I got real respite then because the family assisted me. I was not worried about care for (my son) then because they all care for him.

2 When I go on holiday, which I do to (Caribbean country), I go with my son. Then my family, from my side and my late husband's side will support him and I can actually rest, girl.. In fact some of my church members take him for a few hours or go with him to church functions during the week. Most of them know him and I don't worry when they go with him because they understand how he is and encourage him to participate in whatever they do. That's why I was saying I did not need Local Authority respite services. I am sure government respite will be for a longer time, but the carers at respite do not know my son as well as my friends at the church do, although they will have a care plan. It would just make me worry so much about how he is managing.

3 … the respite centre calls you many times to manage one issue or other. A care plan fails to capture certain details which families have learned to deal with from the childhood of the person with learning disabilities; those same things become major disasters for outsiders/ the community to manage because they are scared of being held accountable. ….. The only real respite we have is when we leave him with his siblings, with my family or my husband's family….they know how to manage behavior or create environments where the behavior does not manifest or how to divert the behavior and get the best out of and for …(my son).. The respite has been reduced to 21 days; is not easy to get and does not really give us respite

4 Well, we were offered respite and a care plan was made for that. I visited the respite centre with my husband and child. We were supposed to leave him there for two afternoons for them to interact with him. He sat down close to the door and did not interact with anyone except to stand up and quickly run out when we came back. From his non verbal signs when he went to the respite centre, we read that he did not like to be there. ….We go on holiday to (European country of origin) with him. Our families look after him while we take a break. We have no worries when family looks after him because they all know him from when he was a child and know how to deal with challenging behavior. He knows all of them and enjoys the attention from both sides of the family….I

would say as a family we were scared of diving into the unknown of respite with complete strangers as it is offered by government.

5   My older sister is 79 and lives in (place in UK), used to look after ... but she has health issues. Her daughter helps me if I want to take respite. There are local authority respite centres but we never used them ..., because it is difficult to get respite and we would rather that family does the caring. ....

6   I have had massage at the CC but could not stay long enough for the healthy lunch. In time, I am sure I will have more relaxation time as my daughter goes to school......

7   The carer respite is difficult for me to organise because ..(The cared-for)... can agree to go today and when the time comes, she doesn't want to go and I cannot force her. I would like to go to (African country).. with ..(my daughter).. I have brothers and sisters who would help me there and I would get to relax but ....(my daughter)... agrees and then changes her mind.

8   I have used the CC carers Respite Flexible Breaks funds for respite. My ex-husband stayed in my house with my son when I went on holiday.

9   Respite is a tricky one. We have two sons. The eldest lives in (European country) with his family, so here, I am by myself. .... finds it hard to interact socially. .... I do not want to leave him with strangers but would love to go to ..(European country of origin) ..on holiday and see the rest of my family. The last time I went was before my wife died. Our eldest son stayed with him for two weeks and we were able to go home.

10   I used the respite facility last year for 21 days. I have mixed feelings about it because I am not sure my sister enjoyed it. (What did you do during the respite?) I was at home with mum. It was also a busy time for my course so I did my assignments and did a bit of spring cleaning of the house getting rid of clothing that is old for all three of us

Table 16: Worry with community access
Participant   Sub-Theme: Worry with community access

1   He has gone on respite for a week and that was one of the worst weeks I remember.......Almost immediately after dropping him off, the phone calls from the respite centre started enquiring about all sorts. I almost wanted to go and fetch my son. I worry about how he is doing.

2   (I thought you said your son went into supported living, how come he lives with you now?)

Girl, ... was thin as a rack after eight months of living by himself. He can't cook, so he was ordering take out. Two months after he moved out of our home, his dad was admitted into hospital. Because of the stress of the next six months when I could not pay him attention, he got into debt, he lost a lot of weight. He moved back home ...

3   ... He lives in a Housing Association. I support him with budgeting but the rent and bills are high and sometimes I use my own money for his groceries. .... So, even when ...(he). is living independently, I worry about many things relating to his welfare and I am always 'on call'. The burden of care just shifts........ Having ....(him)... live independently does not reduce my worrying or my care because I know what he is doing every day and can anticipate where challenges will occur.

(So job wise, you think ... would make a good assistant in such an almost predictable environment?)

Yes, because most of what happens in the Day Centre or other such places are things ... understands. ...Such things make me very anxious. I am all for access to the community for people with learning disabilities but I am aware as a carer that the shifting community access environment presents challenges for people with learning disabilities and the public's perception of their employability. There is need to sensitise employers and the public. (Government policy advocates for community access for people with learning disabilities though?)

 Yes, but the community has expectations which some people with learning disabilities might not fulfill. My son, big as he is, the public expect him to be able to perform and when he cannot, they ask rhetorical questions like,' Are you stupid or what?' My son does not understand why he is being insulted because most of his life has been in environments which have shown him patience, nurturing and encouragement;... What is perceived as public banter can result in challenging behavior and the publicthen question some of the implications of access to the community. I always find myself confronting such comments on his behalf. ......

........So services we have always relied on are being cut off and what replaces them does not meet my need to sit down and chat with staff, which sometimes is the only respite the carer has in between waiting for the Day centre pick up.

4   ... has little speech and he only says the basic words necessary for what he wants only. .. does not watch TV except the football matches. He does not like to interact with many people and certainly not strangers. When he is at home, he sits in his room, he likes sitting in the dark. We have tried changing that but it brings challenging behavior. ....This is why it is difficult for me to take government respite because respite centre staff might not understand when to leave him to do what he wants and then he can be challenging. You see, for me as a parent to be telephoned all the time about the behavior, it is more stressful than if I look after him myself.

5   There is the Day Centre which she goes to.... I had registered her for the befriending service which has since lost funding. It did not work very well because ... did

not understand why the stranger was there. …'s paid carer retired because of ill health and we went through a period of a lot of staff turnover which confused … even more. I resorted to the church and employed another church member whom … knew. In church, it is those people she sits next to most times that she recognises and she is able to work cooperatively with.

6   Right now he goes to a special school and has challenging behavior on the bus.

7   I tried to engage her in activities in the community but she was unwilling to do them and she does not like crowds. Even her siblings have tried but she only goes out in her wheelchair to do a clothing shop once in a while with her sister and comes back quickly after that. She used to go to a Day Centre but that has now closed.

8   He goes to the gym for use of the swimming pool and the football. I think there are other services but we tend to stick to areas where it's safe, challenging behavior wise.

9   He likes the parks and does not like to socialise. My wife used to take him around to try things when he was younger but he was not interested. So whatever there is out there, I am only concerned about what he likes.

10   She goes out swimming, shopping…. needs supervision.. and support…. When she was younger, mum used to take her to church. I have tried but she stubbornly refuses to go most times now.

Printed in Great Britain
by Amazon